Saving Jaguar

John Egan

Saving Jaguar

Porter Press International

First published in June 2015
Reprinted in August 2015
First published in paperback in April 2018

ISBN 978-1-907085-74-1

Published by
Porter Press International Ltd.
Hilltop Farm, Knighton-on-Teme,
Tenbury Wells, WR15 8LY, UK
Tel: +44 (0)1584 781588
Fax: +44 (0)1584 781630
sales@porterpress.co.uk
www.porterpress.co.uk

Designed by Grafx Resource
Printed by Gomer Press

Jacket photo by Tim Andrew

Contents

Acknowledgements

I would like to thank my ex-colleagues from Jaguar for all the help they gave me in writing this book, in particular John Edwards whose timelines anchored the fast-moving action of the book, plus Mike Dale and Roger Putnam who helped me put the Ford ownership into perspective, Mike Beasley for his recollections of our productivity improvements, Kes Lodge for providing the statistics on quality, and Peter Leake and the Jaguar 'Old Lags' whose reminiscences were invaluable. David Littleford, my personnel manager at Specialist Car Division, reminded me of the depth of the anarchy at BLMC.

Philip Porter of Porter Press encouraged me to write the book and has given me help and much-needed support all the way through the project. He has been backed up by his team and I would therefore like to thank Louise Gibbs, Abigail Humphries, Annelise Airey, Sarah King and Leanne Banks.

As to images for the book, I would like to acknowledge all those who have assisted, including Mike Cook of Jaguar North America and Kevin Wood of LAT, plus motorsport artist Graham Turner and the editors of the publications reproduced. Mark Holman and Mark Hughes have very kindly proof-read the text and I am grateful to them. Designer Andy Garman has not only done a first-class job but also overcome a few software challenges along the way. Above all, I must thank my wife Julia who gave me succour through the events in the book and bravely sub-edited my work.

Introduction

The 1970s were a time of great peril for most British companies. Strikes had reached epidemic proportions. By 1978, even national and local government were overwhelmed by this wave of discontent, as everything came to a halt in what became known as the 'The Winter of Discontent'. Rubbish was uncollected in the streets, and even the dead remained unburied.

The Labour Government and their union paymasters had no answers to the anarchy created by their own 'looney left'. The militant shop stewards were firmly in charge. How would Britain – 'the Sick Man of Europe' – ever be governable again?

In its despair, the electorate turned to Margaret Thatcher and her Conservative Party, whose primary promises were to, 'Control inflation and to strike a fair balance between the duties and responsibilities of trade unions.'

Mrs Thatcher was elected Prime Minister by the biggest swing in voting since the Second World War. That swing had occurred mainly amongst skilled working-class voters, who knew from first-hand experience how useless their union leaders had been in curbing the behaviour of their own militant shop stewards.

In 1974, the Labour Government had given a powerful new weapon to the unions – the 'closed shop'. Without union membership in a closed shop, you could not have a job. This completed the powerful hand of cards held by the trade unions in controlling the workplace. Voting was carried out through the intimidating process of mass meetings, strikes were confirmed through brutal mass picketing and, to cap it all, if an individual did not support his local shop steward, he could lose his job.

By 1978, the trade unions had themselves lost control of the workplace to their militant shop stewards, who had seized this powerful hand of cards for their own devices. How would Margaret Thatcher and her Government fulfil their electoral promise? Where could they make a start on what appeared to be an intractable problem?

Well, they owned perhaps the biggest single bag of commercial trouble themselves, thanks to the state ownership of BL Ltd, where 200,000 workers had lost 32 million man-hours through strikes in 1977 – equivalent to 160 hours for each employee.

Michael Edwardes, the BL chairman, had been appointed by the previous Labour Government and had struck up a good working relationship with them, particularly with the Prime Minister, James Callaghan. Edwardes had already made an effective start: reducing strikes, disposing of unwanted assets, closing unproductive sites and halting loss-making activities. The Callaghan Government was extremely supportive of BL taking these actions but also in backing them with new investment.

Almost immediately the new Thatcher Government arrived, they added to BL's problems. Their monetarist policies, employed to curb inflation, sent the pound climbing, rendering BL's products uncompetitive, and making all Michael Edwardes's finely drawn calculations obsolete. To make BL viable in these new circumstances not only were massive further closures and redundancies necessary, but huge increases in productivity were needed.

To add to Michael Edwardes's problems, the philosophy of the new Government was strongly against subsidising loss-making state-owned enterprises. It would demand extraordinary leadership for Michael to emerge with anything out of this maelstrom. Prodigious improvements in quality and productivity were obviously necessary, but some new investment from a very reluctant Government would also be required. I watched this battle royal from far-off Canada, half-glad not to be involved but half-anguished that there were some parts of the concern that could be saved, especially Jaguar.

I had experience within BL and had been able to help create a successful business out of Unipart, in spite of the trade unions and in spite of the bureaucratic sclerosis of the company.

I knew that I could rely on the good sense and self-preservation instincts of the British workforce when having to put in place a revolutionary survival plan. Michael Edwardes had clearly made a good start on changing the attitudes of all employees at BL, but when facing up to the trade unions he would need steely determination from his major shareholder, the Government.

I could see that he was going to get that from Margaret Thatcher, whether he liked it or not.

This was the situation when I decided to take up Michael Edwardes's offer to be the new chief executive of Jaguar, in April 1980. I knew that Jaguar was in the deepest of trouble and that its closure could easily follow those of MG and Triumph.

Chapter 1

The End

1989

The telephone conversation that changed our lives at Jaguar had been strange and quite abrupt. The chairman of Ford of Europe, Alex Trotman, had said he would like to see me. He was going to visit his mother in Dundee and he would like to pop in, to 'talk of things of mutual interest'. I offered to show him round our charming old-world assembly operation, with its crafted leather seats and walnut veneer dashboards; he would have seen nothing like this before. He indicated that this would not be necessary. Perhaps he would like to see our new engineering centre – which I later found out was the equal of anything he had in Ford of Europe. 'No, I know you well enough from your products,' he observed. And that was that. I was worried by the tone of the telephone call. We had had some desultory talks with Ford some time ago, in which they had offered to sell our cars in Germany, possibly under the Lanchester name. But I felt that they would be unsuitable partners for Jaguar. The Ford way was moving metal with grim determination, strictly to the letter of the Ford book. I could find no place in this for Jaguar's traditions of 'Grace, Space and Pace' – as our advertising slogan had once put it.

Three days later Trotman arrived and was quite relaxed – jovial, even – when meeting my PA, Diane. He was wearing a smart tweed three-piece suit, which I thought entirely suitable for meeting his mother in Dundee. This put me somewhat at ease. Maybe there were innocent 'things of mutual interest to be discussed' after all. However, when pleasantries had been exchanged, his demeanour abruptly changed. He looked at a spot somewhere over my head and made a number of staccato points, describing how the Ford Motor Company could be of help to Jaguar Cars. 'We have national sales companies all over the globe able to sell your cars… we have considerable technical skills able to help you… considerable investment is possible…'

There were more points he made. It all seemed well rehearsed and committed to memory. I eventually broke into this monologue with the tentative observation that these were not the sorts of thing we needed right at this time, and began to explain. But he looked at me sharply and said that nothing would become available unless Ford had 'some sort of ownership'.

At that point I clarified matters: Jaguar was not for sale. He seemed genuinely surprised.

'The Ford Motor Company has seven and a half billion dollars in the bank,' he replied. 'Everything is for sale.'

We had a few final words, as he clearly thought that a 'No' from me was not sufficient.

He asked whether I would put the question to my board.

'This is not the first time someone has asked to buy Jaguar. I will put it to our next board meeting in two weeks' time,' I replied. 'But their answer will still be "No" – and in any event there is a government Golden Share in place, preventing more than 15 per cent of the company being in the hands of one shareholder.'

He knew of that but was not sure what kind of impediment it might offer. With that, he was gone.

He did not want to listen, of that I was sure. We had already had extremely gentlemanly talks with Eberhard von Kuenheim of BMW and Gordon White of Hanson Trust and had agreed with both of them that if they did go ahead with their intention to buy Jaguar, the management did not necessarily go with the company – at which point they had ceased to be interested. It had been much the same with General Motors.

But I felt that Ford would not be put off by any such notion. Clearly, only ownership would do, and then Jaguar would be made to do whatever Ford had in mind. As I later pointed out in discussion with Roger Smith, the chairman of General Motors, 'When an elephant gets into bed with a mouse, it probably gives little pleasure to the elephant but the mouse usually gets killed.'

Was it all going to end like this, after all the efforts we had made? This did not feel like the start of anything positive. It had all been too aggressive for that.

We had improved productivity by 400 per cent. We had put the Jaguar XJ6 into the top five in the JD Power customer-satisfaction index. We had 1,250 engineers working in our new engineering centre. Strikes were virtually a thing of the past. Our new 1990 model-year car would overcome all the residual problems of our recently-launched XJ40. We had been profitable since 1982. Our company was virtually a university, so much effort did we put into training and education. We had an exciting new model programme.

What mistakes had we made to end up like this? Of all the companies in the world, Ford would be the least capable of having an arm's length relationship with a luxury car company. It would be fully integrated into the Ford way of doing things. Integration into BL had been a 15-year nightmare, and this putative liaison had already started badly.

I struggled with what to do next.

My instincts were to fight. But what did the rest of the board think? True, I did fear the looming recession in the US, where orders were already slowing down. The British Government was fighting inflation with a policy of high interest rates, and this was resulting in an uncompetitively high value for the pound, and thus low profits on our US sales. I knew we did need technical cooperation to create the economical performance car that global warming dictated. Somebody's help would be useful, but Ford's, from the discussion I had just had, might prove fatal.

Boards are there to make wise decisions, so I thought it best that, together with John Edwards, my finance director, I should put some future scenarios to the board for their consideration. In the meantime, perhaps we should seek potential partners that might possibly give us a somewhat safer home.

Ford of Europe chairman Alex Trotman would not take 'No' for an answer. He was an unwelcome but persistent suitor. (Jaguar North America)

Chapter 2

Before the beginning

1968-74

In 1971 I joined the British Leyland Motor Corporation – generally known as British Leyland or BL. This was when it was not yet too late for an exceptional and courageous management to have saved much of the company. Three years earlier Donald Stokes, chairman of the Leyland Motor Corporation, had in effect taken over the ailing British Motor Holdings, with the full encouragement and backing of the Labour Government, who had given him a modest £25 million loan. The merger brought together on the one hand BMC (the former Austin-Morris combine) and Jaguar, which had merged with BMC in 1966 to form BMH, and on the other the Rover and Triumph marques that had been absorbed by lorry-maker Leyland.

The Government wanted to be seen to be backing businessmen regarded as being winners. Donald Stokes had all the appearances of being a winner and now he was in charge of all the major British-owned motor companies, brought together in what was one of the biggest vehicle manufacturers in the world, with a realistic capacity of around 1.5 million cars per annum. The opportunities for success were simple to describe but difficult to execute – because the forces ranged against him were so formidable.

The strength of BL lay in its market position in cars and trucks, especially in the UK and the Commonwealth, in the US sports-car market, and in the many other markets appreciating stylish products such as the Mini, the various Triumphs and Rovers, and of course the Jaguars. All that needed to be done was to bring each well-regarded make or model up to world-class levels of quality, reliability and productivity, and at the same time build up the financial and engineering resources to replace these successful vehicles. All non-essential operations should have been sold off and all uncompetitive product lines and inefficient or superfluous production facilities, of which there were many, disposed of with some speed. To do this, Stokes would have had to win the hearts and minds of his workforce, without which none of it could happen.

He would also have to encourage the British components industry to do the same; but after all, he was their biggest customer. All he had to do to maintain his market position was to be internationally competitive. I suppose you could have said the same thing about machine-tool maker Alfred Herbert, car maker the Rootes Group, dominant auto-electrics manufacturer Joseph Lucas, electronics-to-defence group GEC, and very many other British industrial giants of the past. But the forces operating against Stokes were many. Strangely, the first was the complacency and incompetence of his senior management: their early post-war success had made them a self-satisfied group, and they lived well. The car park outside a senior management meeting resembled a meeting of the Mafia, with their lines of cars and chauffeurs. Offices and management dining rooms were plush, with the grander ones having wines served at lunch times by liveried butlers.

Management training was carried out in a leisurely way in country castles and retreats, but showed no interest in examining how to equal the performance of the company's rapidly expanding European rivals and, of late, their new Japanese competitors – who were becoming formidable practitioners of process engineering. They probably would not have believed the achievements of their competitors, even if they had been told of them. There was no great appetite for seizing opportunities to radically improve performance, and no significant jumps in quality or productivity were achieved during BLMC's existence. Much of the reason for that lay with these senior managers.

The second enemy was the trade union movement. The unions were considered by the public to be the most powerful people in the land, even more powerful than the Government. They rejected any meaningful involvement in improving the performance of British industry, as outlined in Secretary of State Barbara Castle's innovative Government white paper *In Place of Strife*. They had a lofty and disdainful approach to literally everyone, hiding behind an umbrella of piousness and making out they were warriors against social and financial injustice. But aside from creating industrial turmoil, they were willing to do little to address the industry's waning competitiveness.

Under the same pious umbrella, a frightening force was gathering strength. Militant shop stewards, in the absence of management leadership and union discipline, were gaining control of the workplace. Typically, they were masters of the mass meeting, the extraordinarily intimidating process that unions had chosen as their fig leaf for democracy.

The BLMC shop stewards had created a Combined Shop Stewards' Committee to fight any redundancies resulting from the creation of the new business. Union bosses well knew that 'leaving it to the lads' meant leaving decision-making to these few men – and these men were certainly not interested in the wider agenda of performance improvement and wealth creation.

These problems were endemic in British industry, managers in many businesses despairing at ever again being able to build big projects or run large companies in an orderly and world-competitive manner. Donald Stokes would have been exceptional indeed if he had been able to carry out his survival plan against the wishes of this brutal enemy.

The third enemy was the competition. British manufacturers had enjoyed a quick start after WW2 compared to their war-ravaged competitors in Germany, Italy, France and Japan. The industry was lucky in having some very talented leaders, usually carrying on where they left off in 1939, but with the added experience of having been good at making war products. For example, at what eventually became Jaguar's Castle Bromwich plant, Lancaster bombers and Spitfire fighters had been manufactured on assembly lines which ended at an airstrip, from which the planes were

---

Donald Stokes headed up British Leyland from its formation in 1968 until 1975. First and foremost a salesman, Stokes presided over a period of desperately poor productivity, massive under-investment, bad product decisions and disastrous labour relations. (LAT)

The original Jaguar XJ6, launched in 1968, was Sir William Lyons's final masterpiece and his personal favourite of all his iconic designs. Not only was the XJ6, supplemented by the XJ12, a great success but in evolving forms sustained the business for nearly 20 years.

immediately flown off to their service squadrons. There were no unfinished products cluttering up the factory, a feat we were not able to equal until many months into the recovery programme at Jaguar.

However, these men were not typically gifted organisation people. They were designer-entrepreneurs like Sir William Lyons at Jaguar, or else they were creative engineers such as the team at Rover, while over at the Leyland truck company Donald Stokes was a very fine salesman. At BMC they had developed the Issigonis front-wheel-drive system that would be copied by practically every maker of small and medium-sized cars in the world, but they had not integrated Austin and Morris – which operated not just as separate car franchises, but in some ways as separate and almost rival production centres.

None of the senior figures were organisation men gifted enough to create the systems necessary to run one of the world's biggest vehicle manufacturers. In the meantime, Volkswagen, Renault and Fiat were growing rapidly and organically without the need for difficult mergers, in countries desperate to have work. Even more ominously for all of them, Toyota in Japan was creating the world-class process engineering systems that would eventually be copied by all manufacturing companies in the world. The world was not standing still, and competition was improving by 4 or 5 per cent per annum. BLMC could not afford to stand still. But stand still they did.

All the BLMC car companies had extremely low productivity. This was not just brought about by strikes at the group's own plants and those of its suppliers. There was poor engineering design that made for difficult assembly of vehicles and components, a lack of statistical process control, poor training and an almost complete absence of leadership on the shop floor.

There were also 43 plants in the car-making process, often too small and badly located, hundreds of miles apart from one another. Bodies and components frequently had complicated movements from one plant to the next, adding to cost and confusion. We shall see later that when BLMC tried to bring in Measured Day Work, instead of traditional piecework, it was calculated that the plants were 25 per cent over-manned; in truth, if proper comparisons had been made with the world's best car companies the over-manning would have been closer to 50 per cent. Clearly the resources required to bring engineering and product development up to world-class standards could have been generated if the workforce had been productive. All this could have been seen as a great opportunity; unresolved, however, it would inevitably lead to failure.

Also somewhere between danger and opportunity lay the Labour Government, whose heart and wallet were firmly attached to the trade union movement. As Secretary of State for Employment, Michael Foot later gave legal support to the closed shop, thereby inflicting great damage on manufacturing companies.

Resolution of industrial disputes requiring government intervention inevitably ended up in Downing Street over beer and sandwiches, with patched-up agreements in favour of the Government's friends, the unions. The more thoughtful ministers were aware of the dangers of such behaviour after the bruising they had received with the rejection of *In Place of Strife*. Workplace decision-making was in the hands of the shop stewards. It was no use making agreements with the union bosses, as they were not in charge.

Government economic policy – of whatever political stripe – compounded the problem. Successive governments had varied the terms of hire purchase agreements to control demand, as one of their key weapons of economic management. This had created an unstable pattern for car sales in the UK and the industry's response was to create a similarly unstable demand for employment. Lay-offs and sudden surges of hiring of hourly-paid workers were endemic, creating not only fear and resentment, but also lack of self-worth and skilling in the workforce.

These conditions were easily exploited by the shop stewards. Additionally, governments had used the planning system to control the whereabouts of new factories. The car cities of Birmingham, Coventry and Oxford all had over-employment, with workers flocking to them from all over the country. The Government forced the car companies to expand in Scotland, Liverpool and South Wales, where the collapse of traditional industries had caused high unemployment.

Government economists, in utter ignorance of the true situation, evidently considered that the car companies were massively endowed with managers possessing outstanding organisational capabilities; for that is what it would have taken to create cost-effective new facilities at these remote locations. In the main, these new factories proved a nightmare for their managers; their workers typically hated the discipline required for car manufacturing, and the managers were not capable of providing training and leadership. The motor industry never really recovered from wasting a decade or more of investment.

This policy of 'Industrial Relocation' was almost a death penalty. An alert and resourceful BL management, knowing – one assumes – that it was fighting for survival, should have at least refused to put new investment into these far-away plants and closed inefficient factories and transferred the production to those where it could control quality and productivity, for these were the keys to the future.

A wise and knowledgeable management would have insisted on a massive dowry from the Government for taking the problem of Austin-Morris off its hands. The Government had loaned BLMC £25 million; a realistic demand would have been a £500 million investment. The management of BLMC would shortly rue the day they had taken on such an ailing giant as British Motor Holdings.

At first blush, the top management team seemed to have all the attributes for tackling this formidable set of problems. Donald Stokes was a resilient, cheerful, persuasive salesman. He had a serious and effective manner on television. He was supremely self-confident. John Barber, the finance and planning director, had enjoyed a long career in Ford, the world's second-largest vehicle manufacturer, and was articulate and intelligent even if neither a convincing public speaker nor a born leader. Whatever the vices and virtues of Ford, he surely must have observed at first-hand the processes, systems and leadership programmes which evidently allowed very large groups of people to work successfully in harmony, designing and making motor cars.

George Turnbull, appointed MD of Austin-Morris, had been put in place by Donald Stokes to oversee the successful integration of BMC into

George Turnbull enjoyed a distinguished career in the motor industry, rising through the ranks to be Managing Director of Austin-Morris before resigning to establish a car-manufacturing facility for the South Korean Hyundai Motor Company. (LAT)

the new group – the Austin-Morris division being by far BLMC's biggest operational unit. Turnbull, an ex-Coventry rugby player, was a tough and capable leader, well-liked and universally accepted as a fair arbitrator when sorting out the turf disputes which invariably occurred. In later life, he created the highly successful Hyundai Motor Corporation in South Korea.

What a team, between them combining, as they did, persuasion, knowledge and leadership. How did they do and how did the enemies of progress react?

They cannot have appreciated the peril they were in, doubtless because the company had a 40 per cent UK market share and was making some profit. Their approach as a consequence can only be described as 'business as usual' – but with three distinct added features. Problems of over-manning and over-capacity were not to be answered by direct management action, but by sales growth – an unlikely solution but, on reflection, an obvious one, given that Donald Stokes was a salesman. But of course it was a timorous response to the 'no redundancies' declaration of the Joint Shop Stewards' Committee, and would cost him dearly. Industrial strife was to be solved by the introduction of Measured Day Work as a payment system for hourly-paid workers, to replace the archaic piecework arrangement of payment by results, which British companies had used since the Industrial Revolution.

Finally, a very large central staff was to be built up in London, under John Barber, to guide the operating companies in their search for performance improvements and also to allocate scarce resources.

The operating companies continued as before, often run by the same people who had run them when they were independent. Sir William Lyons still ran Jaguar Cars, but by far the most powerful baron was George Turnbull at Austin-Morris. Ominously, there were no plans to address directly the issues of quality, productivity and shopfloor leadership. There were no plans to close unproductive plants. There were no plans to dispose of non-core activities or discontinue uncompetitive product lines. There were no plans to win the hearts and minds of the workforce, by speaking to them directly. There were no plans to wrest control of the shopfloor from the militant shop stewards. There were no plans to make all the employees of BLMC have the same employment conditions, and grading and bonus structures. There were no plans to add the engineers necessary to design future products to the standards now being achieved by their competitors.

Indeed in its whole life BLMC did not create one successful new product which was better than the one it replaced. 'Business as usual' was not a survival plan. This leadership team was not particularly incompetent. However, to have won, they would have had to be revolutionary in their approach to industrial relations, ruthless in redesigning their business, and would, without any doubt, have needed massive government support for their approach. All of this would have been difficult if not impossible for a publicly-quoted company. Anyone wishing to criticise them has to consider that there were very few business leaders in the UK who did much better.

The large central staff built up in London fulfilled functions usually determined by the staffs themselves. Broadly speaking, there were tasks allocated to the central staffs but they were always open to negotiation, and power remained with the operating units. Resource allocation between companies was bravely tackled by those in London, reports were written and decisions were taken, but these decisions were usually determined by political clout rather than by consideration of future prospects.

As a result, most of the money was allocated to the unprofitable activities of Austin-Morris, even to the extent of developing both a Morris Marina and an Austin Allegro, continuing the nonsense of two competing marques and starving the profitable specialist cars and trucks divisions of new investment. Both these cars were compromised in their engineering, patchy (at the very least) in quality and suffered disappointing sales; they were recently voted as two of the worst cars of all time.

The Government had loaned BLMC £25 million. As previously stated, a realistic demand would have been a £500 million investment. Some investment did, however, leak into profitable product lines. Money was spent upgrading the Triumph plant at Speke in Liverpool and in the new truck plant in Bathgate, Scotland. Productivity and quality, however, continued to be much worse than at their parent plants, and thus the money was largely wasted. A powerful Industrial Relations group was built up at Central Staff, headed by Pat Lowry – a future head of the Government's arbitration service ACAS. He was always decent, thoughtful and humane in his handling of the very many difficult situations that he faced. However, his first big programme, to introduce Measured Day Work, created more problems than it solved.

Piecework was a degrading way to treat a workforce. They were paid only for what they produced, even if the parts were not readily available or were not engineered to fit exactly. So the workers were forced to do progress-chasing and to bang and force parts into place, a practice euphemistically known as Birmingham Engineering, in order to get paid. This was to be replaced with Measured Day Work, offering a decent day's pay for a decent day's work done. In their preparatory studies the planners noted, as mentioned earlier, that by these standards BLMC were already over-manned to the tune of 25 per cent, or 50,000 operators.

The programme had three important defects. The need for shopfloor leadership was ignored. So were the quality defects requiring Birmingham Engineering. But the fatal flaw was that the scheme was site-specific. As it was also rushed, it was quite easy for the shop stewards and the workforce to bamboozle the time-study engineers as to what represented a fair day's work. In most cases it took much less than eight hours to do the day's work, and productivity actually fell. As it now also made comparisons between sites even easier than before, it was not long before the shop stewards realised that they had been given a road-map to mayhem.

This powerful group, having spotted the differences across the BLMC empire, led their members into a succession of vicious strikes to exploit these differences. Anarchy and chaos were in the air, and many senior executives would not or could not visit the shop floor.

The head of Standard-Triumph was one of these. He said that he would not allow the dignity of his position to be undermined by the abusive behaviour that his visit would invite. The shop stewards had immense power through the closed shop. You had to be a union member to keep your job.

This control led to some grotesque working practices, such as night shifts taking their bedding into work to get a good night's sleep. At its most extreme, the Drews Lane axle and suspension plant could do its whole

WW2 Spitfire fighters were constructed at the Castle Bromwich factory that later became a Pressed Steel plant producing bodies for Jaguar. (Jaguar North America)

Sir William Lyons (left) agreed to what he believed was a merger with BMC, run by Sir George Harriman, to form British Motor Holdings. In reality, BMC took over Jaguar and, the business being in dire straits, was subsumed by Leyland Motors to create British Leyland. (LAT)

day's work in four hours, leaving only a skeleton crew behind to clock out. The skeleton crew were paid overtime for these additional duties.

Unbelievably the plant's shop stewards were able to take their members out on strike to defend these absurd arrangements. One huge question had to be asked: where were the managers? Many observers, including government ministers, thought it was possible that these militant shop stewards were in the pay of the Soviet Union. Whether they were or not is immaterial. The results were the same as if they were. A side effect of the activities of the shop stewards tended towards standardising wages, which the craft unions, especially the AEWU (Amalgamated Engineering Workers' Union), hated. These craft unions were very dangerous because they themselves perpetrated and led some of the most damaging long-term strikes.

Even without the stress of a survival plan with consequent plant closures and standardised conditions, BLMC had intolerable losses through strikes. Man-hours lost through the company's own industrial disputes would worsen from 5 million to 11 million by 1974. Suppliers also had their own strikes, of course, causing blackmail settlements.

Whilst management was coping with these almost daily strikes, it had little scope for improving productivity – and, more importantly, making that much-needed leap forward in quality. As we will see later, whilst I was creating Unipart I proved that when trying to improve performance you could take on the militant unions. If you appealed directly to the workforce, they were willing to listen. Because of the scale of the strikes, BL consistently under-supplied its dealers. As well as having an unacceptable wait before their car was delivered, customers were suffering from poor quality and reliability, BL cars often having many times their competitors' failure rates.

But customers and dealers were beginning to have a choice, and ominously European manufacturers were beginning to invade the home market. Perhaps the opening of prestigious Volkswagen dealerships in Coventry and Birmingham, for example, might shake away such complacency?

The new Central Staff, populated with people from Ford or other capable companies, continually reminded senior managers of BLMC's deficiencies, in huge conferences with 300 or 400 senior managers. They would present directives to overcome these deficiencies and assumed that these meetings were sufficient to flush out problems associated with them.

These directives quickly became a cruel joke in the operating units. They were invariably impossible to enact in most parts of the company, because conditions were so different everywhere, resources were too slender to carry them out, or they were simply so impractical that they had to be ignored. In the meantime, every manager had scores of local problems to deal with, for which he did not get help or resources from anywhere.

These directives invited spoof versions. One I remember was entitled 'Reducing Travelling Expenses' and invited managers below a certain grade to hitch-hike from meeting to meeting. Useful advice was included, such as how waiting times would be less at some junctions, and how, if your secretary were attractive, it might be sensible to take her with you!

I coined the phrase 'the reflective layer' to cover this managerial phenomenon: the brains and resources at the top of the company were entirely separated from the problems at the bottom, cementing in the status quo with a ferro-concrete solidity. The spoof version of these missives from Central Office did at least offer useful advice – which was unusual in the real thing. In time, BL settled into an arrangement of two armed camps, with Central Staff seeking change via ignored directives, whilst powerful barons continued to operate in their own chosen way with very little improvement in performance, quality or productivity being evident.

These tensions could have been usefully channelled into a 'fit for purpose' administrative structure. But no serious effort was ever made to use a scalpel to create such a purposeful organisation. It was an outrageously chaotic, but at the same time stimulating, place in which to work. With so much to be done, I found that I could thrive.

Chapter 3

My introduction to BL

1971-1980

I was headhunted by John Barber to join his Central Staff. He was talent-spotting in the motor industry, searching for capable people to help in the immense task of improving British Leyland's performance. At General Motors I had been responsible, together with marketing manager John Neill, for building up the AC spark plug and oil filter business into a fast-moving consumer brand sold through the motor trade and supermarkets. We had been bold and innovative.

At my interview John Barber did not hide the issues. He seemed to have positive ideas on how performance could be improved. I pointed out how weak the financial position was, but he countered that by outlining the huge scope for improvement.

I joined BLMC because I thought that performance improvement was what I did. After all, I was an experienced motor-industry man. I was an engineer and a business graduate. At BLMC I would be with my own kind. At GM my boss had pointed out that if I wanted to be promoted further I would need to work in Detroit and become an apprentice American, as it were. However, neither I nor my wife Julia particularly liked Detroit.

I started work at BLMC in a very positive spirit. They had given me share options and a good salary, and my first company car was a Triumph TR6; true, it smelt of petrol and was full of rattles, but on the open road it had a powerful roar and went like the wind. My first role, in order to get to know the company, was to do profit planning through pricing and cost estimating, as I had done at GM.

In Central Staff I was with a large group of talented and experienced young men, all hired, like me, by John Barber, and all aiming to change the British Leyland Motor Corporation into an efficient and profitable car company. However, the longer people had been in Central Staff, the more disillusioned they had become. Nobody listened to them. They sent directives into the wide blue yonder and nothing seemed to happen. For the ex-Ford people amongst them, this was mystifying. Nobody at Ford would ignore a directive from head office, but at BL this was standard practice. I wondered if there was another way.

My route to stardom owed a great deal to luck. On doing a little background research, I noticed from the published accounts that BL was failing to implement even the price increases allowed by the Government's price-control regulations. All the companies were acting as independent operators, and most of them could have put up their prices by more than the allowed amount, but Austin-Morris and a few others could not. The Government regulations were quite specific: if price increases were all carried out on the same day, a company could vary them around the allowance.

I took my TR6 on a journey to talk to all the finance directors individually and explained that by acting independently, their actions were costing about one per cent of UK revenues or £10 million per year. Regaining this money was probably the easiest £10 million that BLMC could ever earn. My most enthusiastic supporter was David Andrews of Austin-Morris, who had the least to gain but was, above all, a logical finance man. He helped smooth the way for this change.

I set up a simple system for comparing the prices and specifications of our products with those of our competitors, and a clearing house for subsidiaries to bid for the slack to be taken from those not able to take the full increase such as Austin-Morris. Hey presto! We had an 'everybody's a winner' proposal, a system that would regain the one per cent we had lost by having everyone acting independently. Central Staff gained control of pricing because it all had to be done on the same day, the 'barons' gained more money for their plans, and BL gained £10 million in profit. Flushed by our success, my boss Geoffrey Robinson, later to become Paymaster General in the Blair Government, ushered me in to see Donald Stokes. He was extremely friendly and enthusiastic. 'This is Central Staff work as it should be,' he said. 'Now, why did you come to join us, here at Leyland?'

In a not overly-modest reply, I said, 'I thought I would rather like to do your job.' This was met with even more enthusiasm, for he immediately said to Robinson, 'This is the sort of man we are looking for.' In a more serious tone he said to me, 'OK, let's see what we can do to help with this ambition.' Stokes charged ahead, and two or three days later he offered me the job of being MD of Leyland South Africa. This was a very big and complex business with local car and truck assembly, and sales of the whole BL range. It was, however, partially owned by a local entrepreneur, Jack Plane, who was also a director on the parent board.

From my pricing work I suspected that the South African operation had a history of 'Favoured Nation Treatment' in its transfer-pricing arrangements. How good, in reality, were the profits? I smelt trouble. In any event BLMC would win or lose in Britain, but not in South Africa. When I discussed the offer with Julia, she very firmly said, 'No, we are not bringing up children there. Apartheid is not for us.' I declined the offer. Stokes did not really hold it against me, and merely said that there were lots of other things that needed fixing.

A few weeks later I was invited to spearhead the creation of the Specialist Car Division, or SCD. I was given the task of integrating the parts departments of Jaguar, Rover and Triumph. Apparently we would do this first, and at the same time set up study teams to see what other activities could be amalgamated in a similar manner. I accepted immediately.

It was an attractive proposition. At General Motors I had gained plenty of experience running a parts business; Specialist Cars were where the profits would be, and there were large economies of scale to be made, thanks to overlaps of 'ship-to' addresses and part numbers. There were far too many unproductive warehouses, and these parts departments were often badly run; that at Jaguar, for example, was run with such extraordinary

---

The Unipart division of BL was a great success. Advertisements such as this appeared on the back of the company's all-model catalogues during the 1980s. (Jon Pressnell Collection)

UNIPART

FOR ALL YOUR PARTS NEEDS

Unipart replacement parts and accessories are designed and manufactured to Original Equipment specifications for all BL cars, and are fully approved by BL engineers.

The Unipart range covers all servicing requirements, including plugs, filters, oil and antifreeze – and there are thousands of Unipart outlets nationwide, ensuring excellent availability.

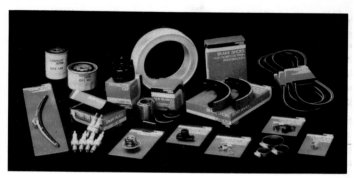

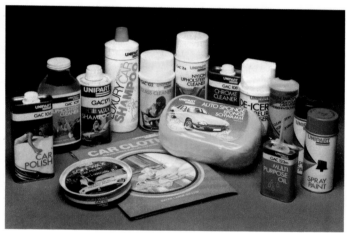

UNIPART

ACCESSORIES – ADDING TO YOUR MOTORING PLEASURE

Unipart accessories give your new car that final touch of distinction and versatility, with a choice of seat covers, auxiliary lighting, sunroofs, car-care items, towing and touring accessories . . . an entire range, from screenwash to trip computers.

Ask your dealer about Unipart accessories for your new BL car – and find out how Unipart can add to your motoring pleasure.

The Answer is Yes. Now what's the Question?

Publication No. 3535/D   Austin Rover Group is a managing agent for BL Cars Ltd.

International House, Bickenhill Lane, Birmingham B37 7HH. Lithographed by The Nuffield Press Limited, Cowley, Oxford, England.

Austin Rover Group

inefficiency that it was even losing money. I had at least the bare bones of a plan.

Everybody was afraid of the plan to create the Specialist Car Division. What would happen if the unions got to know? What mayhem would ensue? Therefore its very existence was put on a need-to-know basis. I was briefed by the putative chairman of the division, Sir George Farmer, the chairman of Rover, but even his own appointment had not been announced. Basically, there was not much of a plan. I had to create the plan and ask the permission of Sir George before I did anything.

Sir George's lack of enthusiasm gave me the impression that his heart was not really in this endeavour. Just as I was leaving, he gave me a warning. 'The parts director of Triumph has been given the job, but he has done very little about it and so you will be replacing him. But because of all this need for secrecy, he probably doesn't know yet.' This was the first time I personally had to sack the person that I was replacing; sadly it would not be the only time I had to do this in the car business.

Everything turned out to be much more straightforward than I could ever have hoped. Nobody was interested, certainly not Sir George, in what I was doing. I had no managerial interference and – much more importantly – no union interference. The brutal and powerful shop stewards at Standard-Triumph, the biggest operation, the ones who had in effect prevented their chief executive from visiting the shop floor, hardly knew where the parts department was situated. Fortunately, too, there were some very capable managers who helped me over the next few months to create a robust plan. The various critical systems of cataloguing, stock replenishment, warehouse management and shipping were quite well done in one or another of the existing systems, and I could shamelessly copy aspects of the more advanced Austin-Morris set-up, for instance, in order to develop a composite system that would improve performance.

The overlap of part numbers allowed us to close some warehouses, the obvious candidates being the Rover ones in South Wales, 200 miles away from the centre of gravity of supplies and destinations. Rover wanted the space and could use the people we freed up. We could promise our dealers big improvements in fulfilment rates and speed of delivery, especially of emergency orders,. And we would have much less inventory and waste, and obviously more profit.

I kept all the employees informed of our plans and our conclusions. I adopted an approach unknown within the company. On walking around together with the supervisors, if anyone had questions, I would answer them and, if a particularly important question was asked, I would gather the whole group together and have an open discussion. It was all too impromptu for the shop stewards to have the chance to object.

This style of management then developed into regular question-and-answer sessions. I personally informed the unions of the huge benefits to customers of the new arrangements, and spelt out the closure plans, the voluntary redundancy terms and the bonuses for staying to the end for those losing their jobs, along with the terms for transferring location. There were to be no compulsory redundancies. I never found the need for them. If the voluntary severance terms are attractive, the uncommitted or unwilling – usually around 25 per cent – will always take them. If that is not enough, there is always the following year.

The shop steward representing the South Wales operations where most work was being lost was one of the most decent and eloquent men I have ever met. His speech arguing against the closures tested my resolve to its limits and challenged me to question whether it was all really worth doing. He spoke for about an hour with remorseless sing-song eloquence, and I was reeling in my chair by the time he quietly finished. This apart, we had no major problems until the final few days, when out of the blue the two shop stewards at the Triumph plant, where we were centralising the clerical activities, indicated that they were objecting to the loss of work elsewhere and to the change in working practices involved in taking on other people's work at Triumph.

Popularly known by their workmates as Batman and Robin, they told me that their members were angry and there was trouble ahead. 'We will see for ourselves,' I said, and immediately organised a meeting of all employees, bussing them in from all three locations. Everything was fully explained again as to why we were doing what we were doing, but more importantly where every single person would sit on Monday morning when they came to work. I noticed that Batman and Robin were in the audience. I asked whether there was anything they wanted to add. They shook their heads.

The merger duly went ahead, with only one further incident. The day of the merger came. It was very cold, and on cue the heating failed in the newly-refurbished offices. Even with the addition of some space heaters, which sent out ghostly blue flames, the offices were still freezing. Yet our employees carried out their assignments as planned. They were there to work, not to strike. They were there to give of their best – if we, the management, did likewise.

I drew some important lessons from this assignment. Improvements for the customer are non-controversial and an easy rallying cry for the business and for employees. Take on the unions to achieve them, and employees will understand and will enable you to achieve rational goals – but do explain your plans directly to the workforce. Employees come to work to do their best, so get top management working on the systems that will allow the employees to succeed. Be bold, as everything is possible if you try hard enough. Finally, it is better to have a plan than fail because you are carrying on with 'business as usual'.

When I had completed the amalgamation of the SCD parts operation, I taught our SCD dealers to become formidable wholesalers of the Unipart range of all-makes parts. I used expertise I had learned at AC Spark Plugs to lead and incentivise the SCD parts managers – a hitherto forgotten group of men – into successful wholesalers. My incentive plan took all the winners to Istanbul, the destination of their choice.

This Unipart range of all-makes parts had been created by Gerry Minch, the Austin-Morris parts director, and was a copy of a similar programme at Ford, his previous employer. Gerry had not seen Unipart as expanding beyond his Austin-Morris empire. He was a hard-charging, hard-drinking legend of the motor trade, and an outrageously profane character, his dialogue being mostly comprised of four-letter swear words. But he was leaving his creation to lie fallow, and his dealers started losing business to mine.

It was really a petty internal squabble, but Gerry cried foul. He had

---

For a period, it seemed as though British Leyland was jealous of the Jaguar brand and, rather than promote and celebrate the great marque, actually gave the Leyland Cars name greater prominence. The irony of this period advert is the contradictory strap line. (Philip Porter Archive)

Michael Edwardes in characteristic pose – and characteristic pin-stripe suit. His robust management style represented a major change of approach and was vital in giving me the support to carry through my changes and initiatives at Jaguar. (Jaguar North America)

Jaguar XJ3.4

Leyland Cars

In a world of changing values a Jaguar is still a Jaguar.

created Unipart and he wanted me warned off and forbidden to compete with him. George Turnbull was chosen as arbitrator. Even though George was Gerry's boss, this was acceptable to me. I arrived at the Kremlin, as the Longbridge headquarters of Austin-Morris was nicknamed, and was ushered into George's office, where Gerry was already ensconced with his many colleagues. George commenced proceedings by asking Gerry to state his case. Gerry started off at a furious pace and continued swearing at me for about 20 minutes in his usual colourful way. The only coherent contribution came from George, who occasionally grasped a word or phrase and repeated it clearly. He eventually summarised the situation by saying, 'Gerry does not want competition. What do you say, John?'

I felt showing a sense of humour might defuse the atmosphere. 'Let me say first of all, George, how much I like coming here to Austin-Morris. Everybody is so polite to me.' George smiled and told me to get on with it. I then pointed out that we only had five per cent of an immense all-makes market between us, and my competition was irrelevant in the scheme of things, and accidental. I was going after much bigger competitors, such as Joseph Lucas. If Gerry would like any help, I would gladly show him how it was done. At this, Gerry's colleagues had to hold him down. George ushered me out of his office and told me to carry on and keep up the good work. Later Gerry was transferred to other duties.

Sadly, very little further work was done to integrate the Specialist Car Division, in spite of our success. This probably sounded the death knell for the weakest brand, Triumph. However, under the leadership of Allen Sheppard, who later became chairman of Grand Met, we integrated all the parts and component operations of Leyland Cars under the Unipart brand name, in a similar manner to my integration of the SCD parts operation.

With John Neill, who I hired from GM, I transformed Unipart into a highly successful consumer brand for the all-makes replacement parts business, and just as importantly into one that was fully competitive with all its world-class competitors in service to dealers and customers around the globe. Whilst building up Unipart as a powerful brand, John and I hit upon the idea of doing something similar to the famous Pirelli pin-up calendar. Our version would have beautiful photographs of scantily-clad girls, shot in superb locations by Lord Lichfield. We felt it was sure to be a successful promotional device in the motor trade and a ready-made way of advertising the Unipart name to a wider audience.

Unfortunately BL's marketing director learned of what we were doing. His ego somewhat hurt, because we had dared to use our initiative, he warned Lord Stokes that the calendar would be bad for his reputation on television, particularly with the elderly ladies of Bournemouth. According to the secretaries' grapevine, Stokes had been heard to mutter, 'If I have a parts director who needs nude girls to sell parts, I will get myself a new parts director…' Forewarned, John Neill and I went to the meeting, with him on his own, with a 30-minute presentation on what an outstanding job we were doing at Unipart. 'Well, Donald, if you are going to sack me I would like you to know who you are sacking and then deal with why you are doing it,' I started off.

'None of that. Just get on with the pictures,' was his reply. 'No,' I said. 'If I am being sacked, we will have to do it my way.' I then started describing the fully integrated, fully competitive business we had created, making £70 million profit per year – almost as much as all the losses he was making elsewhere. He kept trying to stop me, repeatedly saying my job was safe. But no, I kept ploughing on until I had finished the full presentation. 'Your job is safe,' he said. 'Now show me the pictures.' It would have appeared a strange sight to an outside observer, John Neill, Lord Stokes and myself, in his darkened office, intently peering at Lord Lichfield's young ladies. 'But these are very tasteful. Not a single old lady in Bournemouth will be in the slightest bit upset with this,' said Stokes. 'Get on with it, and well done!'

The story typified two things: on the one hand, the internecine warfare between the central staffs and the operators out in the businesses themselves, and on the other the wit and common sense of Donald Stokes.

Whilst I was busily integrating the parts business, BL was hitting trouble. As with many badly-managed companies, they were rapidly running out of cash. They turned to the Government for help. The Government was ruthless and, as with all British governments, absolutely inept in investing in business.

A hastily-arranged report was made by a team led by Lord Ryder of the IRC, the Government's Industrial Reorganisation Council. Help was not on the cards; instead, a transfer to state ownership was proposed. Accompanying this, the report recommended a reorganisation that turned out to be even more of a nightmare than the status quo. For good measure, it suggested a participation scheme with the trade unions that called for goodwill from those least constitutionally likely to offer it, the violently unwilling shop stewards. Faced with the humiliating ultimatum offered by the IRC, Lord Stokes would have been well advised to have handed the keys of Austin-Morris to the Government and continued to run the other profitable parts of the business. I was able to put this idea to him whilst at a management meeting at Quaglino's in Central London, when he and John Barber were telling the top 100 BL managers about the Government proposals. It was in the urinals and he was in the next booth.

I said, 'Donald, give them Austin-Morris and walk away. You'll be making £40 million per year and you'll be a hero.'

He said, 'No I can't do that. We can't break up what we have created.' But he turned away and looked uncertain, and quite anguished. I think the real reason was that he had left it all too late. I do not think at that time he had any other choice. He had committed the cardinal sin of running out of cash. When that happens, you are helpless.

A year earlier he could have negotiated with an interim Conservative Government and might have struck a deal which would have been better for all concerned. But business is about making money out of satisfying customers. BL had neither made money nor satisfied customers. If you are doing neither of these things, there is no particular merit in size. Implementing the Ryder Report caused even more chaos and, until Michael Edwardes arrived in 1978, British Leyland simply spiralled into deeper confusion and ever-increasing losses.

By then the annual time lost to strikes had grown to 32 million man-hours. The structure imposed on Leyland Cars by the Ryder Report was that of complete integration, with no subtle use of the surgeon's knife to extract economies of scale with minimum pain, but instead a brutal dismemberment of the famous brand names.

Thus Jaguar's famous Browns Lane plant became Large Car Assembly

---

Industrial relations in the '70s and '80s were characterised by the picket line where striking union members demonstrated their grievances and attempted to stop the flow of goods into and out of plants, intimidating their fellow workers from crossing the line. (Herbie Knott/Rex Features)

The other regular constituent of the union movement was the mass meeting when workers were harangued with anti-employer sentiment and generally persuaded to vote, in a supposedly-democratic situation, for the ultimate weapon of strike action. (Bill Ellman/Rex Feaures)

Plant No.2; its engine plant became part of the Power Train Division, and all its other functions, including its engineering department, were scattered to the winds. The Unipart organisation continued successfully as before but was given the added responsibility of running the service operation and component manufacturing.

As the Parts and Service Director of BL Cars, I was given the unenviable task of chairing the Product Quality Committee. I could see at first hand the consequences of the company's appalling quality. Dealers were spending hours preparing cars for sale to the customer. There would typically be up to 20 faults per car and then in the 12 months of the warranty the dealership would have to fix many more faults than found on the cars of our competitors. On the other hand, at that point the car became extremely profitable to Unipart, which was making £70 million per annum supplying the service parts and the parts that 'fell off' or otherwise failed. My committee contained all the people within the company with any role to play in product quality, but organisational complexity meant that at least five heads needed to be banged together to get common cause on any single quality problem. I was utterly ruthless in bringing the customer perspective to the attention of these people.

But I was dismayed when one plant director stood up and gave a 20-minute prepared speech, which seemed to have the general approval of all the others present. What could I expect? His plant had suffered daily strikes, and daily shortages from other plants or suppliers who were having strikes of their own. He had hundreds of engineering defects that needed to be resolved. He had stood as much pain as he could bear – and now he had to take even more pain from me. He was almost in tears by the time he sat down, to the applause of his colleagues. I could understand his problem. I attended the top-level union/management participation meeting ordained in the Ryder Report.

Quality and productivity were on the agenda but were never really discussed. These talks were dominated by aimless debates on instances of social injustice brought up by the shop stewards.

I remember on one occasion, at a tea break, I was standing with a group of stewards. One of them remarked to another that he saw that he had arrived in a taxi and not a company car, as practically everybody else had. He was about to explain what had happened, when the rest of his colleagues, almost in perfect unison, said, 'Have 'em out, Mick. Have 'em all out.' As I wandered away, it occurred to me that they were not joking.

These powerful men could, on any whim, 'Have 'em out'.

I decided that if I were to have any future in BL I would have to run one of the core product companies. Leyland Trucks suddenly needed a managing director. I thought that I was the man for the job, but had a most disappointing interview with the new BL chief executive, Alex Park, newly promoted from being finance director and appointed by the Government, which was in effect now the only shareholder. I put my case of having created the only fully competitive part of BL. I thought I could do it again at BL Trucks. He was alarmingly frank in his reply. He was sure that I would be successful in improving the performance of BL Trucks, to the point of challenging him for his job. Why should he allow me to be a competitor for his job? Why would he be so foolish? I had no answer to that. But I felt that BL had absolutely no future under such a leader.

I left BL Cars and had thought that was the end of that but, four years later, whilst I was working for Massey Ferguson in Canada, Michael Edwardes had different ideas. He was looking for people who had been successful in the fierce cauldron that had been BLMC, and first offered me the chance of running Jaguar Rover Triumph, the Specialist Car Division of old.

I turned the proposition down for a number of reasons. My leadership process would be too diluted across too wide a business. Not only that, but Triumph was by now beyond hope. I thought I would be running a disintegrating entity that would have to compete – for limited resources – with the cash-hungry mass-market Austin-Morris division. Putting a cap on things, the UK no longer looked much of a place to try to make cars. But a later offer in 1980 to run Jaguar Cars alone was altogether more compelling.

I had observed Michael Edwardes going about his business: he was bold, he had a plan, and he was not taking any prisoners. For the first time I saw a worthy opponent for the shop stewards; strikes in the year after his arrival had reduced substantially. Margaret Thatcher was Prime Minister, and industrial chaos was not to be tolerated. Cosy chats with beer and sandwiches and giving in to the lads was not her style. But additionally a surprising piece of work had been done by Pininfarina, the Italian styling studio, on the elderly Jaguar XJ6. A good car had been face-lifted into a beautiful luxury saloon. If we could make this car work properly, we could sell it. The salesman in me saw a remarkable opportunity.

Before taking the job, and much against my will, Michael insisted that I had various behavioural tests. They revealed surprising sides to my personality. Michael assured me these were no barrier to employment. He explained that he could interpret the results better than his behavioural scientist could.

At issue was my method of operation. I managed by creating teams of strong-minded individuals on whose advice I could rely. Of course I became reliant on them, because we were functioning as a team. I was not an autocrat, which is what the behavioural scientist thought the situation demanded. Michael was right. There was a need for team builders as well as autocrats. Michael also agreed a deal with me on Jaguar. It was losing money heavily and, without rapid improvement, would have to be closed down. But if we could turn it around, he accepted that it should not remain within BL Cars. Jaguar would have to be independent, but would have to earn whatever independence it got – that was the only way I thought I could control the unions. I was absolutely clear that vague as his assurance was, Michael would honour this deal, and that I could safely work within it.

At the same time that I was completing my negotiations with Michael, the first of his many shoot-outs to the death with the unions was just commencing. All hourly-paid employees in all the car companies had to accept a common five-grade payment structure, with common terms of employment. If they did not accept by a given date, they would be deemed to have dismissed themselves.

It was manifestly the right thing to do, but the aristocrats of Jaguar would now be treated in the same way as the track workers at the Austin plant at Longbridge. I was assured that all was going smoothly, all the same, so I went ahead with a long-planned holiday, skiing in the Italian Alps, well out of reach of any English newspapers.

The original XJ6s and XJ12s were given a face-lift in 1973 and this model was christened the Series 2. Quality was dreadful. (Philip Porter Archive)

No amount of glamour photography could hide the fact that the dumpy Allegro was a regrettably inept replacement for the best-selling 1100/1300 models. (Jon Pressnell Collection)

Chapter 4

The beginning

April 1980

My previous experience had taught me that when it came to being coaxed into change, BLMC – or BL Cars, as it had become – was like a wild, angry horse, and anything could happen. Whilst driving towards Browns Lane, the Jaguar headquarters on the outskirts of Coventry, I was still blissfully unaware of the situation and was wondering how Michael Edwardes was getting on with his re-grading of the workforce, and how the aristocrats of Jaguar, soon to be my aristocrats, would take to the medicine. The shop stewards at Jaguar were more responsible and did not strike as frequently as their fellow unionists did at the other car companies; but when they did, it tended to have been thought out, and thus disputes were much more serious and prolonged.

So far so bad, I concluded when I got there. There was a huge crowd milling around the factory entrance. All the paraphernalia of a British strike was in place – braziers glowing, men linking arms across the gates, cheers when incoming lorries turned tail and left: the whole nine yards. However, it still appeared relatively good-natured. I parked my car and went to investigate. Soon I was involved in earnest discussions with the strikers.

They very patiently explained what it was all about. One man, who had come expecting to work, showed me his bag of tools. 'These are all mine. We are craftsmen – the cars don't really fit together without us helping with tools like mine. How dare they compare us with Austin! They're just fitters there.' I asked what it meant to them that they would have been, in the words of Michael Edwardes, 'deemed to have dismissed themselves'.

One replied, 'They've done everything else to us. Well, let them sack us.'

I was soon sought out by a shop steward. Was I a reporter? 'No, I'm your new chief executive and deputy chairman,' I replied. 'Perhaps you can explain what is going on here.' He drew me to one side. 'This is it,' he said. 'From what I can see, the rest of BL Cars is going to accept the terms and conditions on offer. Why not? They have little to lose. We have our pride here, we build the best cars in the world – or at least we used to – and these boys are never going to accept these terms. "Stuff 'em!" That's what they say, and if that means closing this place down, it means this place closes down.'

By this time many others had joined us. Some were vastly amused at standing there with their new chief executive, 'having a chat' – some even thought that I was Geoffrey Robinson, who had left the same position six years previously. That said an awful lot about the other four or five chief executives or chairmen who had been employed in between.

But the general mood was sombre, even sad. I spoke to many others but began to come to the conclusion that my shop steward had more or less got the situation right. This was very serious. If I were going to be in work for more than a few days, I would have to act. This thing was not going to solve itself. This was not just shop stewards making trouble, this was real trouble with the workforce itself.

I immediately went to the headquarters of BL Cars, now in a modern office block in the centre of Coventry, and arranged an interview with my chairman, Percy Plant. It suddenly struck me that my situation was getting clearer but more ominous by the minute. Percy was an accountant to his fingertips. He hated losses with the cold fury of a conscientious comptroller. Generally speaking, anything losing money that got near to those fingertips got closed down, quickly and efficiently, with little fuss. On a percentage measurement, Jaguar was the most loss-making of all the BL car companies. The strike could conveniently bring those losses to an end under Percy's expert fingertips.

'Percy,' I started, 'we are in real trouble. The workforce is not going to accept this grading structure. I think I'm as good a judge of these things as anyone. They simply won't do it, as things stand.'

'It's not your problem,' Percy firmly replied. 'Best go home and await events.'

I told him that I didn't want to be the only chief executive of a car company never to make a single car. 'I well know that Michael will not back down, and from what I have seen and heard at the factory gates, neither will this workforce,' I said.

We talked our way round and round this dilemma until Percy himself surprisingly offered a solution.

'Look, left to me I think we can both guess what will happen. Why don't I stand aside and let you go and try to fix things? You go in there as chairman, to fix up this company; you are new, and you are getting some independence. You are all they have got, but at least it's a bit of a chance, and they might grab that chance as better than nothing. But you must get them to accept the grading structure as it is. If you try to compromise in any way, it's the end for you as well as the company'.

It was worth a bash, I thought. 'If you can fix that, Percy, I'll go and give it a try,' I said.

Percy checked with Michael Edwardes, who also thought it was worth a try – but that, as discussed, I would not be allowed to compromise any part of the grading structure. So, newly promoted and having discovered an easier way into the factory, alongside a personnel man, Ken Edwards, who was deputed to help me, we met Bob Knight, Jaguar's chief engineer and the company's MD. Bob had been fighting a rearguard action against the rest of BL Cars ever since Geoffrey Robinson had left, trying to hold on to the semblance of a company in the hope that at some time in the future Jaguar might be recreated. Bob was deeply pessimistic, not only about the grading dispute, but about everything else too. He was a dedicated and persistent chain-smoker. He puffed and he thought, he puffed and he thought.

I could see he was slowly coming to the conclusion that I was an agent of

---

Ken Edwards (top left) became my personnel director and company secretary. However, like most of the team, he was also an engineer. Bob Knight was a pre-eminent engineer, who fought long and hard for Jaguar Engineering to remain a separate entity within BL and thus kept the Jaguar name alive. He was, though, a reluctant manager. (Philip Porter Archive)

I was greatly heartened by the passion of the visiting members of the Australian Jaguar Drivers' Club. From left: Cliff Rattray-Wood, Bill Heynes and Les Hughes. (Les Hughes)

the devil. In any event, our two positions of MD and chief executive were laden with ambiguity. I don't know how much, if anything, he had been told about my appointment, but it probably wasn't very much, judging by my previous experience of BL. Bob had been forced to put up with all kinds of nonsense from his superiors. Was I just more of the same, but likely to be frighteningly persistent and too close to hand? Could we make it work? I was poking about with a white stick. He was a very fine and meticulous engineer and heaven knows we were going to need all the good engineers we could get. I was never a slave to organisation charts, and I offered to make it work, with me as chairman and him as MD, concentrating on the chief engineer part of his role, while I concentrated on the rest.

He puffed and he thought, and puffed and thought, and he said he would consider it. But he did not want to get involved in the grading dispute. He would certainly leave that to me and to BL Cars. He left me very much with the impression that he was going to leave the company, which he did a few weeks later in spite of all my efforts to dissuade him. He made it very clear that he was tired of fighting Jaguar's corner and that the whole thing was looking pretty hopeless from his point of view – or indeed from any point of view.

I then sat down with my manufacturing director, Mike Beasley, and Ken Edwards, who I had promoted to personnel director. I had only been at Jaguar for four hours, but I was already needing a personnel director, and his reputation was sound. Harry Adey, the Browns Lane personnel manager, was also present. Time was short. Not only did we need to get to know and trust each other, but we had to get something moving before the whole thing became too bitter to be resolved.

I had a powerful group here. Mike was ex-Ford, capable, efficient and had been at Jaguar for eight years. He had no illusions about the problems facing us. Ken was extremely canny. He had seen everything before, nothing surprised him, and he was our oldest dog – as wise as he was experienced. Harry was a former shop steward, a poacher turned gamekeeper.

Harry was tricky, hardened to the ways of the battlefield, and in reality the ultimate architect of success in what was a street fight. He started us off.

'John, don't think for one minute that this workforce will give in. They are beginning to think that Jaguar is finished anyway, they are so demoralised. They don't particularly care one way or the other.'

Mike then filled me in on the problems of the Castle Bromwich body and paint plant, where things were out of control. Every single body had to be repainted at Browns Lane, with the factory's own outdated equipment, because the paint finish was so bad. What was more, they could only paint red, yellow and white. Mike bitterly pointed out that the yellow was intended for the new Rover SD1 and was unsaleable on the facelifted Jaguar XJ6. Beautiful as it was, this luxury car could not take yellow.

'I think I have got to know Michael Edwardes pretty well. He is not going to give in. His grading structure is far more important than Jaguar,' I added. 'He has only just started his fight with the shop stewards. He can't give in – and certainly not at the start. He has to fight on until he has created a different kind of company, one *he* controls, not the shop stewards.'

After we had discussed the issues from every direction we could think of, Harry again made the running. 'As unlikely as it seems, and as unpalatable as it might be, there is only one way forward. We have to get the shop stewards to recommend a return to work, on the basis that John's appointment as chairman with a mandate to recreate Jaguar as an independent company changes everything. We could very well have a future, so now is not the time to give up.' On this rather tentative basis, we decided to go forward and get the shop stewards together. We planned the details to get all the delegates to a meeting early next morning. As the strike had been declared official, these delegates would have to include an official from the TGWU (Transport and General Workers' Union), the biggest union. This was considered something of a setback, because he did not like Jaguar.

I called in to see my reluctant MD before I left. He was still puffing and thinking. I told him of our plan, if that is what you could call it. In the midst of his misery, he could see the point of what we were doing. 'But can you solve the paint problem? Can you get the money for a new engine? Can you get the money for our new car, the XJ40? The men need hope that there is a future. Can you tell them any of these things? I never could, because I never knew.'

Late that night I drove home battered, bruised, promoted, but with a very uncertain future, even more uncertain than it had been in the morning. But maybe Bob had given me a script for our meeting with the unions. The following morning brought the news that the various car plants were caving in and that the big Austin-Morris factories were returning to work.

Soon our Jaguar plants would be out on a limb, a dangerous place to be, as that was when bloody-mindedness could take over. Our make-or-break meeting commenced with a comedy turn from the union official. He had turned up with a cardboard cut-out of Michael Edwardes, and he stood up, proclaiming that I was a cardboard cut-out too, and they all might as well talk to the cardboard Mr Edwardes as talk to me. I noted a stirring amongst the shop stewards – a change in body language. Perhaps they felt that this flippancy had no place in discussions to decide the future of their company.

I started by making my position clear. 'I am here to recreate Jaguar Cars as a successful independent company, and have agreed my approach with Michael Edwardes – that Jaguar will have as much independence as it deserves. There is no choice but to accept the grading structure as it stands. I am afraid that the common grading structure is part of the survival programme for BL Cars as a whole; anything is better than the current chaos. I have been brought back to save Jaguar. I know that I am capable of doing this, if together we take this opportunity of giving Jaguar a chance. I know how big the challenge will be. I spent time yesterday talking to the troops and I well know how frustrated they are. If we are successful, then in the future we can create our own systems, but for the moment it is as it is.'

This generated further waving of the cardboard cut-out of Michael Edwardes from the union official, but the Jaguar shop stewards called for a discussion break. They later asked to continue discussions but this time without the official. Over the course of two days the discussions went on and on. The offer powerful enough to divert 10,000 people from their chosen suicidal path seemed not to exist. Harry Adey was clear in his own mind what was really at issue. 'They are trying to make up their minds as to whether they can trust you or not. Don't forget that we have had some

---

Uniquely an outside design studio was retained to update the style of the XJ saloons and, by common consent, Pininfarina did a fine job. (Philip Porter Archive)

One of the major sources of Jaguar's poor quality was the paint process at the Castle Bromwich plant, which was then owned and operated by BL. Red, white and unloved yellow were the only colours that could be processed. (Philip Porter Archive)

cynical bastards here as chairmen – some that nobody would trust, and for good reason.'

Whatever else was said, I was the only new ingredient. My track record at Unipart was an open book: nothing had been done there other than what I had said I would do, even though it might have been uncomfortable at times. It was always as I said it would be.

Eventually, after a particularly bruising meeting, where I had expounded my theory that we could sell the XJ6 if we could make it work, the shop stewards told us they would give my ideas a chance and recommend acceptance and a return to work. But they wanted us to book a cinema in the centre of Coventry. They would then talk to the workforce, in groups of five or six hundred. They wanted them to sit down comfortably, and in a mood to listen to a very difficult message. Talking and voting went on all day and back came the shop stewards with the news that, extremely narrowly, they had voted to accept the grading structure, but it was so close that there was no time for congratulations, and it was more a case of dressing wounds.

And so Jaguar lived on…

Many years later, one of the stewards confessed that the vote had actually gone narrowly the other way, but that they, the shop stewards, had collectively decided that it was in the best interests of the workforce to return to work, hence the remarks about dressing wounds.

I got a taste of the difficulties lying ahead when a couple of days later I was completing my rounds of our factories with a trip to the assembly lines at Browns Lane. It was three o'clock in the afternoon, a full hour before the shift ended. The first group of operators was sitting down, talking and drinking tea. 'So this is how we compete with the Germans, is it? Sitting on your backsides? Why the hell did I bring you back from the strike? You might as well have stayed outside.' With this and other tirades, I strode down the assembly lines, gathering a crowd behind me. But with a full hour to go, literally no-one had been working.

'I won't go and fight for the investment that this company needs if you stay on your fat backsides,' I said. 'Either you must work or we will close this place down.' I was struck by how little excuse was given. This was clearly the norm, but this norm was not part of my survival plan. Every hour had to be worked, even the last one. But at least I was talking direct to the workforce.

That first week did have two silver linings to it. On the Friday, a coach drew up outside my office and a group of 20 or 30 people got off and went into the factory. On enquiry, I found out that they were a group from the Australian Jaguar Drivers' Club, spending a holiday in the UK, the highlight of which was a trip round the Jaguar factory. I arranged later to have lunch with them. In a voice shaking with emotion, the leader of the group described how much they enjoyed and appreciated their visit to this 'hallowed place' and thanked me most sincerely. 'Gosh,' I thought, 'if this is the effect Jaguar has on at least some of its customers, we really might have a chance.'

Finally, I went to see Sir William Lyons, the founder of the Jaguar company. I wanted to have his support for our endeavours. To have his name on our new letter-heading as the president of our company would add distinction and legitimacy, even though we had not earned much of either yet. The offer surprised him, to the point that his Lancashire roots came out. 'Eeh, lad, I'm already President,' he said. 'Didn't anyone tell you?' From this shaky start, I gained an ally. For the next five years, he gave me his advice and support. No matter how extreme our problems became, I knew that we could sit down together and puzzle our way through. His insights, especially into strategy and product design, helped me to be clear and decisive. Nobody could have had a better mentor.

Chapter 5

First Steps

April – September 1980

Clearly Jaguar had no future if we could not fix the Castle Bromwich body and paint operation. Having to repaint every single body and having only three colours did not indicate much of a future for such a famous luxury car. Completed in 1940, the plant itself had an illustrious past, having been built by William Morris, Lord Nuffield, as a purpose-built factory for the large-scale manufacture of the Spitfire fighter plane. After a wretchedly chequered start, it had gone on to make nearly 12,000 Spitfires – more than half the total built. There is a memorial in the middle of the factory, dedicated by the workforce to the airmen and squadrons who had flown their aircraft. I remember attending a very moving ceremony in 1988, when Air Vice Marshal 'Johnny' Johnson, the RAF's leading WW2 fighter ace, re-dedicated the memorial on the 50th anniversary of the making of the first Castle Bromwich Spitfire, to the extraordinarily haunting sound of the V12 engine of a Spitfire being flown overhead.

By the 1970s Castle Bromwich, now owned by Pressed Steel Fisher, had become a jobbing shop, making 'bodies in white' – unpainted bodies – for various car manufacturers, including Jaguar and Triumph.

The background to this was that in 1965 BMC had taken over Pressed Steel, and merged it with Fisher and Ludlow, which it had acquired in 1953. This had been one of the reasons that Sir William Lyons folded Jaguar into BMC: he was afraid that Pressed Steel Fisher, as a near-monopolist owned by a rival company, might make difficulties over the supply of bodies.

At a later date BL Cars had added a paint plant. Unfortunately, this used what was intended to be the company's new standard paint process, known as TPA – short for 'Thermo-Plastic Acrylic'. This had been created by General Motors and was a low-cost process which melted the final colour coat at very high temperature to create a high-gloss finish. Bill Lyons had never over-invested when creating a new car, and he usually spent as little as possible on tooling for the 'body in white'.

So from the very beginning, lead filling had been used by Jaguar to cover the blemishes in the 'body in white' that were inherent in low-cost tooling. This was especially the case around the beautifully sculpted headlamps, and sadly the high temperatures used in TPA were very close to the melting point of lead, resulting in the lead and paint running into each other. In the badly led and poorly motivated Castle Bromwich factory, this technical issue proved to be literally a show-stopper. The plant blamed the poor tooling, while Jaguar rejected every single body and reworked and repainted every one. This was the situation I had inherited.

The seeds of the solution were sown by the ending of manufacture of the unloved and loss-making Triumph TR7 sports car. At this point Castle Bromwich had only Jaguars to make. Solving the technical issues inherent in the TPA process meant little to Austin-Morris, the volume-car arm of BL, which had ended up inheriting the plant. It was losing a great deal of money, making only 15,000 bodies per annum in a vast great works capable of making many times that number. There was a strong argument that BL would be better off closing the plant and being done with it.

Yet to Jaguar Cars the continued operation of Castle Bromwich was a question of survival. I had read somewhere that the characters in Chinese for 'crisis' were a combination of the two characters for danger and opportunity. I learnt very quickly in the turnaround of Jaguar that when we were in extreme danger, I had to search carefully for the opportunity. The danger was obvious: Austin-Morris clearly wanted to close the Castle Bromwich plant, which was of no value to them. For Jaguar, however, if we could fix the plant, we would have unlimited body-making and paint capacity. The paint plant at Browns Lane had only ever had a total capacity of 30,000 cars and thus this was the limit of car production there. The lowest-cost option for Austin-Morris might, in fact, be to give me the plant.

Austin-Morris was run by Harold Musgrove, a man I had quickly identified as the one BL Cars senior manager to be reckoned with; he had started as an apprentice at Longbridge, and was now chief executive. He was the man who had sacked the notorious 'Red Robbo' – Derek Robinson, the chief Longbridge shop steward who had led over 500 walk-out strikes in his three-year term of office. Not only had Harold sacked Robinson, but he had also won the vote at a mass meeting of 20,000 men called by the unions to defy the sacking.

Harold had been made 'Midlander of the Year' for his launch of the Metro, later becoming President of Aston Villa football club. He was a hero of the Midlands. He was a hard, uncompromising man, doing the most difficult job in BL. It was strongly rumoured that for relaxation he and Andy Barr, his director of manufacturing, chewed the heads off whippets in his office after work.

I interrupted a few weeks of wrangling, blame-chasing and fruitless meetings to visit Harold and try to get a resolution of the body plant issue, which was clearly my biggest problem. There were no whippet heads lying about, and we had a very calm and dispassionate examination of the alternative solutions.

'John, don't take this plant on,' he said. 'The unions are amongst the most difficult to deal with, your people have no experience of body shops, and TPA is a pig of a paint process. If we can't solve the problems, you won't be able to do so either. Let me close the plant and build your cars for you in Longbridge…'

It was an interesting proposition, but not one I judged realistic. 'I don't think that any other workforce but Browns Lane could build our cars,' I replied. 'They are more hand-crafted than precision-built. No, I think that if Jaguar is to survive, there's not enough time to do anything other than improve the current process.'

Harold let me have my way. 'If you really think that, then there's no other choice. You take the plant, all its overheads and workforce, and the best of luck to you,' he said. 'But mark my words, you'll waste a lot of time and trouble at Castle Bromwich. I'll give you three months before you give up, and I end up making your cars for you at Longbridge.' He shook my hand and wished me luck. Over the years in all my dealings with Harold, he was always trustworthy.

A few days later Mike Beasley and I were walking through Castle Bromwich, taking possession of our vast new plant. We seemed like squatters, the Jaguar body and paint operations taking up only a small part of this once vibrant place. As we walked around, we grew increasingly gloomy. We could not find anything that appeared to work. The stampings themselves, before they were made up into a body, were poor; we thought even the original sheet steel must have been blemished.

We would need to bring the Jaguar body experts over from Browns Lane to do the cosseting and buffing up before attempts were made to paint the body – as they had done in the past, before there was a paint plant in Castle Bromwich. Exquisite process controls would be necessary to tame the paint process. This was supposed to be a difficult plant from a union point of view, so how much change was possible and how quickly could it happen? From out of the blue Mike said, 'I haven't seen a single black face in this place. Have you?'

Whilst we were summing up with the plant manager at the end of our visit, Mike sought an explanation for the lack of ethnic minorities.

'Well, the unions vet the applicants before our employment office takes them on and, as you can see, they don't send up very many black people,' was the rather testy reply. Luckily we had brought Harry Adey with us.

'That's against the law,' he pointed out. 'We can't run a plant with a colour bar. Not only is it illegal, but it is absolutely against everything we have promised our people at Jaguar. This is going to stop and stop right now.' Mike Beasley immediately weighed in with his support.

'You'd better bring in the shop stewards straight away,' he said.

After they had all trooped in, we explained our position.

'Castle Bromwich stands a small chance of survival and that requires Jaguar fixing all its technical problems and then growing the business to the point where it is viable. But we are not doing any of this if you continue to break the law. Now here is my offer. We employ whomever we choose to employ, from tomorrow onwards, or we bring in the police to find out who has been breaking the law, and encourage the police to prosecute them. That is the offer, but it doesn't leave you with much choice. It's either us or the police…'

There was then a rather subdued general discussion about the chances of the new management fixing all the technical issues surrounding the plant. Mike had already made up his mind to bring in experts from the manufacturers of the paint plant, and the manufacturers of the paint itself. There was at least some hope in the air. Eventually the shop stewards offered to help and – surprisingly – even to try to support our robust ideas on whom we employed.

From this rather grim beginning, the Castle Bromwich unions tended to be amongst the most supportive of our efforts to improve the performance of the company. The trade unions at Castle Bromwich were not as bad as everyone had made them out to be.

On assuming control of the plant, we immediately stopped production. The cars were virtually unsaleable anyway. We reworked all the unfinished vehicles we had on hand to bring them up to as good a standard as we could manage.

In the meantime, we allowed the task force of experts to painstakingly examine all the processes of manufacture at Castle Bromwich, and bring them under control. It was possible; it could be done, but it was going to be very difficult. We had to put infinite care into making the body far more accurately than ever before, in order to lessen the amount of lead needed for rectification. We even had to go to British Steel and demand better sheet steel, and then invest in some better tooling for the presses, change the paint formulation and control the TPA temperatures to a very small range that flowed the new paint, but not the lead.

We had to redistribute our workforce between Castle Bromwich and Browns Lane, particularly encouraging some black employees to join us in breaking down the colour bar. The experts arranged a full palette of paint colours for us to experiment with, and thus we added to our unfortunate trio of red, yellow and white shades.

After this traumatic period, and after we had restarted production with good if not perfect results, the task force of experts recommended changing the method of painting. They recommended going from TPA to the process which all other grown-up luxury car makers used – an additional clear coat over the base colour, instead of melting this to give the required high-gloss finish. I thought that I was a risk-taker, but this astonished me. Against the

---

Harold Musgrove (top left) was one of the good guys with whom I could do business. (Jon Pressnell Collection) Mike Beasley was manufacturing director and then assistant managing director, and a close ally

The XJ-S, which was based on the XJ6, replaced the legendary E-type in 1975 and was more a grand tourer than sports car (Philip Porter Archive

odds, we had survived, but now they wanted me to put everything up in the air again. We did make the change, but not for some while.

During my very early days in the job, I realised that metaphorically we had numerous 18-inch shells in the air, coming at us with great speed, and all capable of sinking us without trace. Two had missed – the grading dispute and the Castle Bromwich paint plant. I now had to turn my attention to a third shell. As yet, we had no separate accounts for Jaguar, but I knew that we were losing money at an alarming rate. The sale price of our cars did not even cover our variable costs. We were only selling 15,000 cars per annum – only half the break-even level – and we had taken on the costs of a huge new plant at Castle Bromwich. We were probably losing about £50 million per year or about 30 per cent of net sales, which is about as bad as it gets.

I needed a finance director and a break-even plan before everybody lost patience with us. I offered the job to John Edwards, a colleague of mine from Massey Ferguson. I knew we were going to have to move swiftly, and I was looking for somebody who I could trust to get on with building up a new organisation, creating a plan and keeping the heat from BL off us. But above all I needed somebody from whom I would take good advice, especially when I was in danger of making a wrong decision. I knew John had all these qualities. He would turn out to be a stout advisor and as tight with the money as if it were his own.

The nearest shell closing in fast was product quality. I appointed a purchasing director, Pat Audrain, to be our evangelist with the suppliers. To be our 'St John the Baptist' with the dealers, we appointed Neville Neal as our service director. Neville was a real gentleman of the old school, and proved his worth within days.

During one of our very early crisis meetings, my PA, Diane, came in to say that there was a customer complaint, out of the ordinary, and one she could not deal with – and she dealt with difficult customers far better than I did. She was a tower of strength and as valuable as any manager. Her news was that there was an Arab businessman at the gates of the factory with a TV crew, and he was threatening to burn his 'useless' car. I sent Neville off to deal with the matter. A few hours later, with the agenda of our meeting not yet completed, Neville returned, quite forgotten in the turmoil, smiling benignly, but slightly the worse for wear.

'Well, what happened? We heard no fire engines,' we all asked at the same time.

'Well, we are now very good friends,' he said. 'He is on his way back to London. I'm going to fix up his car and, failing that, I have promised him a new car. I did some National Service in Egypt and we both remembered Cairo and we both have an interest in brandy. I took him off to a pub to discuss that, and his problems with the car. He seemed quite happy when I put him on the train to London.'

The TV crew had dispersed and we continued with our meeting. However, we did reflect on the fact that angry as people were, when complaining to us – even as dramatically as our Arabian businessman – all they really wanted was for this beautiful car to work. We decided that we would try to save every customer who did complain, no matter how expensive the solution. We decided that the very act of complaining was an invitation for us to behave well, and if we did, the customer could be satisfied, and return.

A few days later I was packing up my papers and having a moment of reflection when David Fielden, the quality control director, came to my office carrying an armful of components and wearing a very worried expression. It was yet another 18-inch shell, as yet unexploded. Just before I arrived at Jaguar, some cars had been suffering under-bonnet fires associated with the fuel rails of the fuel-injection system, especially on our V12 engines. The general conclusion was that these had been caused by the deterioration of the fuel hose. The supplier had suggested a replacement hose, which was the component being fitted in a current recall of 40,000 cars.

David had not been satisfied with the solution because he considered that the Lucas-designed fuel injection was simply no good. It was, he said, 'Heath Robinson in conception and likely to leak'. He had been closely monitoring the situation, with an eagle eye on the warranty returns. He had also been doing some further experimentation with the new fuel hose, and discovered that although the inside of the hose was very stable, when the outside was exposed to fuel over an extended period of time it deteriorated quite quickly.

In other words, we were recalling the cars to put them into a state potentially more dangerous than before. The reason for his current state of agitation was that he had just been notified of the first under-bonnet fire of a recalled car. Now we were in real trouble. If we recorded six of these incidents, we would have to inform the US authorities and be obliged to organise a full recall; but as we did not have a safe recall position, we would have to advise customers not to use our vehicles.

There could be no worse situation for a car manufacturer.

Underneath David's arm, however, he carried the solutions used by all our competitors. One in particular, employed by Porsche, was simple, beautiful and very unlikely to leak and, most importantly, not protected by patents. We set off straight away to bypass our original designers and suppliers and to design, prototype and test our own solution. I well remember visiting the so-called testing 'laboratory' – a wooden lean-to shed with Jim Randle, our new chief engineer, and several worried-looking young men earnestly trying to simulate harsh under-bonnet conditions on a shaky rig that itself looked likely to fail at any time.

This seemed an unlikely place to be trying to secure the future of our company. I resolved that, as soon as it were financially feasible, we would have better engineering facilities. In the meantime, I had a most unsatisfactory interview with the sales director of Dunlop, the supplier of the fuel hose. He aggressively asked how we were using the hose. 'Well, it does say on the drawing – that your chief engineer has signed – that it is to be connected to the fuel rail, and thus clearly carrying fuel, for the fuel-injection system,' replied Jim Randle and David Fielden in unison.

'It rather usefully says "Fuel Hose" on the outside,' I pointed out, before saying that I expected Dunlop to pay for any resultant recall.

That was actually the least of his company's problems. What it did not want was for us to continue using its fuel hose with the design as it was; but that meant that we were on our own. How wise David Fielden had been to set us off on a wholly new engineering solution. As a courtesy, I phoned the head of Porsche, whom I had recently met, hoping that he did not mind us using his engineering solution. No, he did not mind, but something in the tone of my voice must have portrayed anxiety, because he did offer his help. I was surprised, but in turn all of our German competitors were surprisingly helpful whilst we were struggling with our early efforts to survive. It was disarming, and I felt very encouraged: even our competitors seemed to want us to make it.

We had a number of very anxious weeks as we tested our solution, arranged a production fix, built up stocks, and embarked on another recall. The anxiety was raised a few more notches when Jasper Carrott, the famous Midlands comedian, suffered one of these under-bonnet fires on his own car. What a turn he could have made of this, but in fact he was very kind to us – a true Midlander – and never mentioned a word of it to anyone.

I gathered my newly-formed management team together to make a formal analysis of our position. I felt that we had some growing confidence; we had overcome three big problems, all capable of destroying us, but I knew that 'business as usual' would not do. To survive into the long term, we needed to understand where all the big problems were, where all the 18-inch shells were coming from – anything that could sink us. Our survival plan had to be comprehensive from the start. Of course, we could not do everything at once, but we could try to do things in the right order.

The score sheet we emerged with looked something like this:

Quality – faults in the first year of warranty

Jaguar:	18	Mercedes-Benz:	6

Productivity – cars per employee

Jaguar:	1.25	Mercedes-Benz:	6

Education – university degrees

Jaguar:	78	Mercedes-Benz:	3,000

Product Engineers

Jaguar:	200	Mercedes-Benz:	1,000

Profitability – percentage of net sales

Jaguar:	minus 30 per cent	Mercedes-Benz:	10 per cent

Strikes

Jaguar:	many	Mercedes-Benz:	hardly any

The conclusions we drew were these.

We were looking for a radical change in behaviour and performance, and the place to start was with quality. It would be non-controversial with the workforce, it would be the right lever to change behaviour, and there was no need for ambiguity: we could concentrate all our programmes on one goal. We also knew from our work on the Castle Bromwich paint plant that 'right first time' quality made for huge gains in productivity. But other things were also clear.

A massive training programme was required, and we obviously needed more product engineers. Clearly we did not have enough engineers to create a new car, although we were supposed to be designing XJ40, our XJ6 replacement. On the other hand, we were not free agents, as we were losing money at such an alarming rate. We would have to do something to stem the flow, but whatever we did, while doing it we could not compromise

The board of directors in the early days of my time at Jaguar. From left: Mike Beasley, Bob Berry (marketing director who soon moved on), Ken Edwards, myself with a Series 3, David Fielden (quality director), Neville Neal (service director) and John Edwards (the financial director with whom I worked closely) in front of the old main office entrance at Browns Lane. My office, which had been Sir William's, was on the first floor, to the right.

our quality planning. For the moment, the only action we would take on productivity would be the boost we would get from 'right first time' process improvements on quality. We were very conscious of not wishing to introduce any ambiguity into our message to the workforce.

Now we had John Edwards on board as finance director, we could start addressing our losses of about £4 million per month, to give ourselves a stable financial platform. In 1980 we lost over £50 million on sales of £150 million or over 30 per cent of net sales, possibly a record for a car company, I thought. John created a matrix with all costs in descending order of magnitude on one axis, and on the other axis we rated each cost-related activity in descending order of importance to our quality programme. Clearly those large costs that had little impact on our quality programme had to bear the impact of our cost-cutting.

Our collective decision-making tended to be pragmatic and inventive. For example, our fifth biggest supplier was Gardner Merchant, our caterer. We subsidised our canteens, and managers had free lunches; the system produced friction in spite of its vast cost. I was particularly anxious for change after one of the shop stewards had come to my office with his bacon sandwich, complaining that there was insufficient bacon. I decided that I was approachable, which was good, but I did not want to take on the duties of a food controller.

We put the contracts out to other major caterers, with very poor results, but on widening the net we found a local entrepreneur who had a quite breathtaking solution. He would match existing prices in the canteen with his own takeaway menus, but he would create supermarkets selling sandwiches, salads and – more importantly – a selection of groceries. He argued that with almost 3,000 women working at our factories, if his prices were keen enough he could get their weekly grocery shopping too.

At the same time the managers lost their free lunches. This was the master stroke, as even the shop stewards thought that this action was selfless beyond duty. This was a very good programme, as it reduced the catering cost to zero and saved 12 per cent of our annual loss.

We tackled our suppliers to reduce their costs, with mixed results. More imaginatively, we declared that any component failure rate of more than one per cent in the first year of warranty made that component of unsaleable quality, and the supplier would have to pay the dealer's labour charges to fix the problem.

We also triggered a voluntary redundancy scheme, paid for by BL head office, to ease off the payroll the head-count freed up by the 'right first time' quality process improvements. In other areas we had to add employees. We needed more engineers to achieve our quality improvements and to make a start – even if token – on our XJ40 new car programme. At this stage, it was more of a morale-booster than a real programme. We also had to start investing in what eventually became a massive training scheme. For the moment, at least BL head office could see that we were trying. This took some of the heat off us and we could put all our efforts into improving quality.

This had to be our obsession.

Chapter 6

Quality

1980-81

I had studied some broad-brush research on income size and distribution throughout the world economy, and had come to the conclusion that half the people in the world who could afford to buy a Jaguar lived in the United States.

The BL Cars North American sales company had once been a class act. At one time, during the height of the US craze for British sports cars, it had sold around 70,000 cars per annum. Graham Whitehead, their president, was the doyen of the car importers in the US – once, in visionary pose, appearing on the front page of *Time* magazine. He was a serious businessman. In later years, one of our billionaire US investors, who owned banks and movie studios, said of him, 'If I sent down to central casting for someone to be president of Jaguar Inc, Graham is the guy whom they'd send'.

Graham was also an amusing raconteur. I remember his story of being an apprentice at the Wolseley company in the late 1930s. He was one of the team given the job of finding all the components to rebuild the four-seater Gyrocar, an extraordinary gyroscopically-stabilised two-wheeler designed by Count Shilovsky, an eccentric Russian nobleman. Wolseley had built the car in 1913, but the Count had subsequently disappeared, and in the early 1920s the car was disposed of by burying it several feet under the ground in a corner of the factory. But just before WW2 Shilovsky reappeared and announced that he was calling in to collect his Gyrocar in a few weeks' time, and hoped to drive it away. The car was duly disinterred, after something like 16 years in the ground, and Wolseley set about restoring it to working order. Graham's efforts to collect all the parts, make sense of the drawings, and make the Gyrocar work, was a truly classic story, beautifully told.

But the glory days of BL North America were over. After the antiquated MGB and the unfortunate TR7 had been discontinued, the organisation now had only Jaguars to sell. In common cause, Graham and I began work on what was in effect a shared survival plan. It was almost like having our own Jaguar-controlled sales network. No-one else in BL was interested.

If we could quickly raise the quality of our cars to a saleable standard, we would have a decent network to enable us to sell into a market of unlimited potential. As with the Castle Bromwich option, I was again reminded of the Chinese characters for the word 'crisis'. The danger was that in 1980 the network only sold 3,000 Jaguar cars, and lost a lot of money, so it all might collapse. On the other hand, the facelifted XJ6 was much admired in the US and if we could make this beautiful car work, the opportunities were huge.

I needed an all-embracing and indisputable barometer on which to base our quality efforts. Our own warranty information was filtered through the dealers, and only went back 12 months. One fundamental problem was that our UK dealers were too forgiving of our appalling quality levels, overlooking faults and even fixing or ignoring others without telling us. As a result, warranty figures were too unreliable to be our prime source of information. I wanted information straight from our customers – and particularly from the customers in our most important market.

Graham and I elected to use the JD Power organisation to carry out six-week, 12-month and 36-month surveys of 1,000 US Jaguar customers, and to do similar surveys, using significant sample sizes, of the customers of a key competitor, this usually being Mercedes-Benz.

The first set of results made daunting reading. To be competitive over the three-year period, we needed to resolve, at least to a one per cent failure level, no fewer than 150 fault codes. Nothing less than the entire efforts of all our employees, suppliers and dealers, at a level of intensity and focus never seen before, would do.

There were four distinct problem areas: supplier defects, Jaguar manufacturing and assembly, poor engineering solutions, and poor dealer practice.

Surprisingly, for me at least, the majority of the fault codes related to supplier defects. Our senior management elected to take on five or six suppliers each to deal with. However, as we were aware that many of the suppliers had insufficient engineering resources, we had to build up hunting teams of product and manufacturing engineers, supporting our buyers and senior managers, to help the suppliers, in what would turn out to be a culture change for many of them. In the meantime, to make an immediate improvement, we turned the 'Goods Inwards' department into an immense testing and inspection factory.

I took on the worst five supplier defects, measured by failure rate, myself.

By far the most important and unreliable component was a steering pump made by Adwest. Even after failing a considerable number on our regular pre-despatch road tests, over 40 per cent failed in the first year of warranty. I later learned from one of our Royal Family customers that he always carried a tin of hydraulic fluid with him to top up the pump reservoir when necessary. I was extremely embarrassed to discover that our customers had needed to acquire so much technical expertise.

My team of experts surveyed all the components, and the manufacturing and assembly methods, and prepared a plan of action for the Adwest management. They strongly suspected, however, that long-term reliability required an upgrade of all the seals and recommended changing to Dowty's aviation-grade seals. That would be expensive, but nothing could be more expensive than replacing 40 per cent of the units. However, the expensive seals would be of little use if they were damaged by imprecisely-dimensioned components or clumsy assembly. To produce a high-quality product, Adwest needed to spend a lot of money and revolutionise its ways.

I put all this to Frank Waller, the owner of the company, a very charming and courteous gentleman, as we walked round his plant with the group of Jaguar engineers/experts.

First of all, he was not aware of the extraordinary failure rate of his

---

US chief Graham Whitehead believed, supported and delivered. Originally, he headed up BL in the USA but became a pure Jaguar man and was a key figure in the turnaround. (Jaguar North America)

Addressing a meeting of US dealers. They had to be convinced that Jaguar was not pulling out of the American market and that their quality concerns were being acted upon. (Jaguar North America)

component. Secondly, the amount of money we expected him to spend would possibly be more than the original cost of the company to him and, lastly, he had bought Adwest the company more for its property assets than anything else.

He and I went to his office at the end of the visit. I could see that he was undecided as to what to do.

'Well, Frank, I have to put it to you that if Jaguar is to survive you will have to fix this pump. Its failure rate makes our car virtually unsaleable,' I told him. 'We really don't have time to find and engineer in a replacement. Our survival is in your hands. We think you could be up and running with an excellent pump within weeks, if you try hard enough,' was how I put it.

From Waller's perspective this was not a convincing argument. 'But you can see it might not be my most profitable option,' he replied.

'I can only give you the facts and rely on you to help,' was my rejoinder.

'This is more of a duty call than a business decision, but I will fix it for you,' he said and this was how we ended the meeting. Frank Waller went to it with great zeal. He personally saw to it that our quality methods were immediately introduced and within a relatively short time we had zero failures on road test. We were on our way, and I was sure that longevity would follow with the new Dowty seals.

The second supplier I tackled was Joseph Lucas, who furnished most of our electrical components. I was so daunted by the scale of the task that my first initiative was simply to go to Robert Bosch, the equivalent German company, and see if we could replace the most troublesome components with their parts. The people at Bosch listened to me courteously and impressed me with their excellence, but declined to help. At first I thought it was a cartel and that Bosch did not want to upset their friends at Lucas, but I later understood that their real reason was that they did not think that Jaguar would survive long enough to make the operation worth their while.

So I had to fix my problems with Lucas the hard way. We made a presentation to their senior management, describing all their components and their astonishing related failure rates. Most were worse than the one per cent figure failure rate that triggered the reimbursement payment of our dealer's labour to replace the component. Our JD Power data from the US made it obvious that their Lucas parts were responsible for a significant proportion of the difference between Jaguar and Mercedes-Benz failure rates.

I also knew from my time with Unipart that the Lucas business model was to make little profit on original equipment sold to the vehicle maker but huge profits on after-market sales to the customer, when the car was out of warranty. Each of these deficient product lines was a survival problem to Jaguar, but was very profitable to Joseph Lucas. But if they killed us with their appalling quality, they would not have an after-market at all.

In any event, the Japanese business model was one of excellence without any failures at all. How long could Lucas continue with their traditional and shockingly complacent business practices? It was a legitimate question, but that did not mean I knew how all this was going to play out. I wondered if Jaguar was simply too small to affect the way Lucas did business.

First of all, they seemed genuinely surprised at this itemised account of all their failures and, as I had expected, Lucas did consider that these were profitable products, and thus not a problem to the company. That was enough to make me pessimistic, but I was disarmed by the response of their chief executive, Tony Gill. He was genuinely concerned. Lucas had the ability to change, he said, and they wished to take common cause with us.

Of course the company had a BLMC-type problem of getting plant directors, product engineers and finance men to pull together to fix individual products. But Jaguar's product engineers and the excellent data they gave us meant no-one had any place to hide. Lucas engaged a higher gear, and I was genuinely impressed on my first plant visit. The plant director took me into the works, and my heart sank when I entered a 'dark satanic mill'. However, he stilled my concern by his eager anticipation of what I was just about to see, for in the distance I could see brightness. A large banner proclaimed that 'Jaguar Quality Starts Here' and all the operators were in white overalls, the floor was white and the atmosphere was that of an operating theatre.

Here they had made an effort. I did, though, point out the contrast between the two parts of the factory.

'No,' he said. 'This is the way it is all going to be. It's the only way we will be able to compete. It's just that we've started with your products.' I did hope that all his colleagues shared his commitment, as we needed a huge effort from Joseph Lucas, who supplied so many components to us.

This whole episode did, however, leave me rather puzzled, even though immensely relieved. Why had it not been done before? Why had it taken so little persuasion on our part and how could we have unleashed so much effort? By comparison, my next two products were very straightforward. For some strange reason the door handles of the XJ6 were durable chrome but, at precisely where your fingernails scrape the surface to grasp the handle, there was no chrome but a simple black-painted finish, perhaps saving four pence per car. This component had a 100 per cent failure rate: every single handle eventually became scratched and unsightly. I took my team over to the Black Country factory where they were made. The owner was waiting for us when we arrived. He did not want to criticise the design, but he did want to demonstrate that his factory was capable of high quality.

He did not like the door handles on his own Jaguar and he had replaced them with ones that were fully 100 per cent chromed. However, if we wished to keep the integrity of the original design, he could replace the paint with black chrome, which would be more durable. He had samples ready, and as soon as we gave the word, new supplies could commence. A few days later, after testing, we had our non-scratch door handles on production cars. I had only had to ask, and pay the four extra pence.

One of the UK's most distinguished motor correspondents told me that when recommending to friends whether to buy a second-hand Jaguar, he always told them to look at the door handles to tell whether it was an Egan-Jaguar or not.

He was a little premature, because it was one of the first components to be improved, and we had a long way to go in other areas. The second easy one was the radio aerial. I was too quick off the mark and changed the electric motor for a more powerful Japanese version, but this turned out to be unnecessary. With the improved structural integrity of the body, as we steadily improved our performance at Castle Bromwich, we found that even the old motor was adequate to bring the aerial down as well as push it up - they had quite simply been catching on the internal bodywork.

The same issue formed part of the problem concerning my final product, the GKN differential in the rear axle assembly. For some unaccountable reason, some of them whined; these were not failures as such, but they were a cause for complaint.

The GKN chief engineer, Howard Wyman, had been my rugby captain at school. He came with all his graphs and much paraphernalia, but the fact that I knew him well made his difficult message easier to cope with. I was by now used to great success in these supplier forays, but this time there did not seem to be a straightforward answer. We seemed to have an unhappy combination of an axle vibration setting off a resonance in the body that made things worse. Would our improving levels of body construction integrity automatically resolve the trouble, or merely highlight it?

In the end, action from both parties provided the answer. GKN did, however, put huge effort into improving the accuracy of their own build and assembly processes. We did the same. The problem slowly went away.

My board colleagues and I had rapidly made huge strides very quickly in terms of our supplier-quality programme; so much was true. But a serious omission was my failure to insist on suppliers adding to their engineering resources. We had spoon-fed them with our own resources and solutions, but their deficiencies would come back to haunt us later.

Now to Jaguar's own problems. In parallel with our efforts with our suppliers, we upgraded our own internal approach to leadership and quality. I brought in an acting coach from the Royal Shakespeare Company to teach all senior managers how to lead meetings of large groups of people, and how to make training videos for regular training courses for all our employees. We did not all turn out to be John Gielguds, but we all improved our performance and some of us became polished performers.

Our method of attack was to get senior managers to review all in-house major processes, such as 'body in white', paint, engines, assembly and trim manufacture, to make sure that they were all capable of excellence. When they were, we could delegate manufacturing process improvement to supervisors and quality circles. As soon as we knew that results were reasonably predictable, we could grind out improvements as we went along. We regularly stopped production and had training sessions for groups of 200–300 employees. All quality circles had a session each day to plan improvements to their own quality, and also to raise items requiring help from others. Managers were expected to deal with these requests for help on a daily basis.

Michael Edwardes had appointed an ex-MoD brigadier, Charles Maple, to head up a BL-wide quality improvement programme. I wholeheartedly embraced this initiative. Maple was a colourful character with a most dramatic presentational style. He always made his opening presentation with a bayonet by his side and when he came to the point of how to deal with recalcitrant suppliers, he would show 'how to put it up 'em' with a suitably extravagant gesture. He explained his Quality Index system, which quantified build quality in a disciplined process with an end product marked for defects out of a perfect score of 100. He helped us mark our latest cars and we were dismayed to find that, even after all our hard work, they failed even to score zero.

Everything was measured, every variance reduced and everything improved. A typical but most rewarding example was our effort to prevent water leaks around the windscreen. Our initial decision was to test every car for water leaks, and repair those that did leak, an expensive and time-consuming process with the repair never as good as 'right first time'.

The hallelujah moment came after many months of effort. The lady supervisor of the windscreen-fitting section had been plotting the rapidly declining variance in the profile dimensions of the windscreen aperture in the 'body in white' coming from Castle Bromwich, and had been comparing these against the variance in dimensions of the glass windscreens, which came from two suppliers. If we eliminated one of the suppliers, the remaining one now matched our aperture exactly. She concluded that we could now assemble the two together perfectly and most likely we would no longer need to have a water test. That was her conclusion. As luck would have it, the best dimensions came from the cheaper supplier. The total savings were of the order of £5 million per year.

We were very happy indeed to pay the savings award to the supervisor and her team. Making the body to consistent measurements and to a higher quality and improving the structural integrity of the body were the key to quickly making a huge number of very important manufacturing process improvements. The longevity of all moving parts was strongly influenced by having the dimensionally correct integrity of the bare bodyshell.

An equally rewarding improvement concerned wind noise. Up to this point in time it was assessed on road test by the driver and adjusted by the fitters on the 'final line'. This meant that once the car had been rectified

The V12 engine, here in later 6-litre form, was a magnificent power unit but was excessively thirsty, which needed addressing. (Jon Pressnell Collection)

Ineffective door seals were one of the many quality problems that we resolved. Here a door receives an electrical systems check before it is fitted to the body. (Jon Pressnell Collection)

it had, of course, to be retested. Our solution was to redesign the door seals but test them on the 'final line' with a sonic device. At first, we had inexplicable results until we realised that one of the fitters was partially deaf to the sounds of the sonic device.

There were literally hundreds of these solutions, mostly created by the foremen and their quality circles.

The Quality Index system allowed us to delegate assembly quality, feeding it back down into the system, with each supervisor gaining control of his or her own patch.

We had introduced a bonus scheme as a result of the Michael Edwardes BL-wide system of common grading, and terms and conditions of employment. The scheme could trigger additional bonus payments of up to 15 per cent of salary. But not only had efficiency to be satisfactory, the QI had to be over 50 per cent. Our workforce would become impatient now if we did not get there in line with the other BL Cars plants – and we were starting from the rear of the pack. We were winning, but it was slow; every part of the car needed its windscreen story. There were literally hundreds of supervisors leading teams, and they all had to get it right. But at least there were the bare bones of common cause in the bonus system.

The third category of problems resulted from poor engineering solutions. In the main, these were a gift. Penny-pinching had prevented the old management from adding to the cost of the car by doing things properly, because Jaguar was losing money. This was of course utterly dishonest, from my point of view. How could you charge $30,000 for a car with defects that could easily have been put right?

Overheating was a problem in hot weather, as fan capacity was insufficient. We added a further fan.

The tyres developed flat spots from standing on the dockside during shipment to the US. We changed to higher-quality Pirelli tyres, which were hysteresis-free. Suddenly our wheels were round and the owner could experience the magnificence of Jaguar's suspension system.

The onset of early rusting was eliminated by the application of a robust lining of preservative to all body joints.

This last item came as a gift from BMW. I had invited myself to their engineering centre. All my working life I have found that high-quality companies are so proud of their achievements that they are happy to show people – even competitors – around their facilities. Learning from the grown-ups has for me always been the quickest and most effective way to learn. Eberhard von Kuenheim, BMW's chairman, welcomed me. He was aware of my prime concern on quality and gave instructions that I was to be furnished with engineering solutions to any problems that I raised. On the problem of body joints, I left the engineering centre with tubes of 'goo', an applicator and instructions on how to use it.

One more off our list of 150 faults.

Halfway through our quality programme, when we thought we had something to show for our efforts, Graham Whitehead, the BL Cars North American president, and I decided that I must visit the US dealers and give them hope, before we lost them all. We needed their whole-hearted commitment to a later retro-fit programme for the key quality upgrades we were developing. This would go down well with the customer bodies, whom we thought might very well stay loyal to the Jaguar brand, if we treated them well. We also needed to choose a subset of the old Jaguar-Rover-Triumph dealer body to represent Jaguar. We wanted to keep only the best, but they were going to need a reason to stay.

We arranged five regional meetings. The atmosphere at the first in New York was funereal. I went round the room whilst the dealers were assembling, feeling the mood. BL had in the past treated these people shamelessly. The shabbiest blow was when they had been invited over to see the MG plant, as part of a celebration of MG's 50 years at Abingdon. Whilst they were still in England, a shock announcement was made that MG was losing so much money that it would have to close. Only recently they had been told that the Triumph TR was also going to be discontinued – just when a new V8 convertible version had been introduced, and there was hope that sales might at last pick up for North America.

'What's he here for?' I overheard one dealer say.

'Don't know, but it won't be good,' another replied.

'They just tell about closures over there, and over here,' another pointed out.

Everybody was moody and morose, and they fully expected me to be announcing Jaguar's withdrawal from North America.

I started my presentation by saying, 'I have only one programme and that is quality.' I could feel a sigh of relief from the room. 'Our engineers, management, workforce and suppliers have only one programme and that is quality. We have only just started, but I hope you have noticed that you now have a range of colours including silver, blue and British Racing Green. I have, on pain of death, forbidden the man with the yellow spray gun to use it ever again.' A cry of 'Hallelujah!' went up from the audience.

'We have introduced our North American dealers to the round tyre,' I went on. There was a spontaneous round of applause.

The gathering started taking on the atmosphere of a Deep South revivalist meeting, as I went on to recite all that we had done, such as, 'We have introduced our North American dealers to the radio aerial that comes down as well as goes up.' Roars of approval kept bursting out, even if a particular whistle of disbelief met the news that the door seams would be rust free with the next shipments. I then went on to predict the timetable for removal of all the other faults yet to be fixed.

'To help us all in this endeavour, our suppliers are paying for your labour if the fault rate is more than one per cent,' I continued.

At this point I was interrupted by an incredulous voice enquiring, 'Does that include the Prince of Darkness?'

'Who do you mean by that?' I replied, as if I did not understand.

'Why, Joseph Lucas of course,' he replied. 'The only lighting company that tells its customers to be home before dark!'

The meeting broke up into a series of Joseph Lucas jokes, such as, 'Why do the British drink warm beer?'

'Because Joseph Lucas makes the refrigerators,' was the immediate reply. It was the usual stuff, but a sad reflection on a company that had been making car lighting since the earliest days of motoring.

I then went on to say that in the spring of 1981 we would do a retro-fit of the most customer-unfriendly faults, and I would value their advice as to which problems should be included. A very sensible discussion followed, which pointed to leaving the choice to each individual dealer, a discretionary arrangement. I then went on to say that we would make our big sales push in October 1981 with the 1982 Model Year cars – which would include a less gas-guzzling V12 engine and a relaunched XJ-S sports coupé.

This last announcement met with gasps of astonishment.

'You mean to say that you're going to launch '82 MY cars with everybody else, in October 81?' they responded with an air of incredulity. The record of BL had been lamentable in failing to launch their revised cars at the beginning of each model year with the new model year legislated changes, in line with everybody else in the industry. Instead of October, they would arrive the following March or April, meaning that the dealers had to heavily discount their cars for half the year, as nobody in the US wants last year's model.

I then finished my presentation by inviting them to come to Coventry next year so they could see for themselves the changes we had made.

By the time we got to the last meeting, in Dallas Fort Worth, the dealers were excited. Here was a 'Man bites dog' story – a British car company serious about its quality. The dealers were now warming to what we were doing. Gene Fisher, the Dealers' Association's chairman, promised that if we delivered on our promises, 'Every man jack of the best dealers will be over to see you in Coventry to put in their orders for the 1982 MY cars.'

At the close of my visit I took stock with Graham Whitehead, together with Mike Dale, the experienced and highly professional sales and marketing vice-president. Mike was built in the truly heroic mould, being a fearless leader of his dealer body and an equally fearless pilot of vintage aeroplanes during his weekends. Even he was impressed. We all agreed that the meetings had given us a chance – we three could smell the excitement in the air. If the dealers could tidy up the market after the MG and Triumph withdrawals, and carry out the customer retro-fits, and if for the 1982 season we could deliver a competitive XJ6 and revitalised, less gas-guzzling XJ12 and XJ-S 1982 MY cars on time, then maybe we might just make it.

Up to this point in time, rather than hope, I had only had a sort of dogged determination, almost as though it really was an impossible task I had taken on. But hope was too big an idea to accept. The US dealers had changed all that. Their enthusiasm had been infectious, and made me want to try even harder. I felt I had to make sure that I had impressed on Joseph Lucas – my biggest and most notorious 'problem' supplier – that we were both on a survival mission, and that they really had to deliver.

I also decided to visit other markets where I had some traction with BL's export arm, such as the Australian market, where the sales and marketing director used to work for me at Unipart. I needed to spread the word about our quality and product programmes, before we lost the best dealers.

Maybe we could lift our sales, once we had got our cars to saleable quality, to pull volume through fast enough to survive.

Chapter 7

The turnaround survival plan

1981

After I had been at Jaguar for almost a year, we received our very first positive customer letter. It was from the owner of an art gallery in Chicago.

'I bought my Jaguar as a beautiful sculpture to put outside my gallery. Imagine my surprise when I discovered it worked, and worked very well indeed,' he wrote. Apparently he had been to a Connors v McEnroe tennis match that did not finish until the early hours of the morning and it was bitterly cold. His friends' cars would not start. His Jaguar did, and he had very smugly driven them all home.

Up to this point my PA, Diane, and I had only had to deal with 'irates'. She was much better at this than I was. Her favourite line, which I much admired, was, 'If you continue swearing at me, I won't find out what's wrong and then I won't be able to help you.' But we now started to get encouraging noises. It was evident that our customers wanted us to succeed, and were beginning to like our cars.

A few months earlier, when I discovered that police patrol cars did over 10,000 miles per month, I had placed 30 or 40 XJ6s at very keen prices with various police forces. In one month, I could effectively reproduce one year's hard use of a car in the hands of a customer. These cars had now done over 30,000 miles each and were holding up very well indeed: the cars were becoming much more reliable. Dealers were reporting better build quality, and were even beginning to sell cars to their friends.

Our engineers had, of course, spent most of their time on our quality-improvement programme, but at nights and at weekends Jim Randle, our chief engineer, with a band of enthusiastic senior 'skunk workers', had put together a new-model programme. The most immediate result was a fuel-economy enhancement to our magnificent but thirsty 5.3-litre V12 engine. The new high-compression 'Fireball' cylinder head would take our V12s out of the most penal rates of the 'gas-guzzler' tax levied in the US and this would enable us to relaunch the XJ-S in that market. We would rename the car the XJ-S HE, the initials standing for 'high efficiency'. Almost with our tongues in our cheeks, we had also advanced our plans for an all-new aluminium six-cylinder engine, the AJ6, and for our XJ40 replacement for the XJ6 saloon.

We had put all this to the BL board, and it had all been approved, but to bring realism to the various boards of the BL companies, Michael Edwardes made us go to the Government individually and ask for our money. My team met Norman Tebbit, the Secretary of State for Industry, and asked for £100 million for our new-model programme. I only discovered much later from Michael Edwardes how much we owed to Norman. He had received instructions from the cabinet that as a price for further subsidies BL was to close the worst loss-makers. We were top of that list. Therefore we must have sold our ideas well.

We were only selling the *concept* of the new models, as we had done so little work on them, but we were, more importantly, selling our belief in the future of our company. I have no idea whether Norman saw through us or not, but we were losing serious amounts of money, albeit at the reduced rate of less than £3 million per month, and here we were asking for £100 million to build a new car. Why should the Government have this much faith in us – or indeed any faith at all? Yet Norman gave us approval with a somewhat sceptical but encouraging nod. My management team came away from the meeting a little shocked that we had the money, encouraged that it gave us a future, worried as to what we had let ourselves in for... but absolutely determined to do our best, even if we ended up in the stocks.

My plan for the company turnaround had been to do everything smoothly if somewhat slowly, to allow our 'right first time' quality programmes to drive up productivity slowly, gradually releasing members of the workforce through our voluntary severance scheme, as we became more efficient. We would bring our US dealers over to the UK in early summer, and then relaunch Jaguar in the US with the 1982 Model Year cars – arriving on time, demonstrating improved quality and boosted by a rejuvenated XJ-S at the top of the range. The hoped-for increased volumes and better quality would trigger the bonus scheme. We might get to break-even during 1982.

Michael Edwardes and the BL board listened kindly to my strategy. They were very pleased with our quality improvements and were once again driving Jaguars themselves. But we could not continue to lose money. The £100 million given to us by the Government was for our new model programme, not to finance losses. Any thoughts that the Government money was an immediate passport to sunny uplands could be swiftly abandoned.

The board wanted a plan that showed us breaking even during 1981 and profitable by 1982. If we could not achieve this timetable, we would have to close Jaguar down. They would, however, fund a much enhanced redundancy programme from central resources, to help trim our workforce. I would have to report our progress to the board on a monthly basis until we were profitable, or we closed down.

The discussion was conducted in a friendly and supportive fashion, but there was no mistaking the steel behind the advice. It was down to me to deliver, by pushing down our losses – and quickly. As I drove back to Coventry, I decided that I would trust in the stability of our improvements in manufacturing quality and go for an immediate reduction in headcount. At least I would go out in a blaze of action, rather than die without a viable plan.

Our management team quickly absorbed the implications of the BL board's strictures. We would have to reduce headcount by 20 per cent or even 30 per cent and increase production and sales by about 50 per cent. Further cost savings would have to be made, because we also needed to add at least 300 more product engineers to get on with the new-model programme. It all

Norman (now Lord) Tebbit was an influential member of Mrs Thatcher's Cabinet and crucial supporter, who gave us a vital lifeline with a £100 million Government loan. (ITV/Rex Features)

We involved, and motivated, the employees as much as possible and I presented various awards every month. Particularly effective was the United States Dealer Award. (Philip Porter Archive)

added up to more than a 100 per cent increase in productivity.

The whole thing was obviously going to be much more of a gamble than I had hoped. I had not wished to have a large redundancy programme – this would hardly help our quality. But sales were not going to pick up quickly enough to avoid de-manning. On the other hand, we were getting better at talking to the workforce. The quality programme had required two-way communication right up and down the management structure. We were running large set-piece meetings between the shopfloor and senior management and we had faced few disputes over the previous months; the workforce appreciated regular work. We were talking directly to them and they were listening.

We thus used all our new-found communication skills to deliver another hard message. We could not afford to pay everybody on the payroll, which would have to be reduced by at least 20 per cent, but there was at least BL's improved voluntary redundancy programme. With this, survival was possible. Our cars were improving and our better line-up for 1982 could deliver the volumes needed to trigger the bonus system.

In a way, we were bribing people to go and bribing them to stay.

A clear decision could be made, whether to go or stay: all the facts were to hand and clearly stated in a letter from me to all employees. We would let everyone go who wanted to go. There was no confusion put there by the shop stewards. Everybody could make up his or her mind. Each individual could decide at home, with all the facts having been clearly spelt out.

I was extraordinarily surprised by how well the plans worked. The shop stewards did not know what to make of it all, and were confused, which was always a good sign. I opened my remarks to them by saying that we were in the business of creating 7,000 good jobs, rather than trying to hang on to 9,000 bad ones. We could survive, and we did have the capital for a new model, but if we continued to lose money we would be closed down. By now nobody double-guessed Michael Edwardes. If he said that we would be closed down if we were unprofitable, that is what everybody knew would happen. Enhanced redundancy terms were there for all who wanted to go, but only if they went now; that might not be the case if we had to close down later. I also made it clear that we would only release people at a rate that did not compromise quality. This was absolutely vital to protect the jobs of those people remaining.

The true Jaguar believers stayed and the faint-hearted went, including many shop stewards. This did blunt the union message. The shop stewards were also genuinely anxious not to prevent any individual losing out on what was a generous settlement. I thought they were more worried about that than anything else. We began losing people at the rate of 500–600 per month. When about 1,500 people and many shop stewards had gone, there seemed to be a genuinely easier atmosphere, a more workmanlike tempo. Surprisingly, the Quality Index began to rise above zero. I felt in my perambulations about the plants that there was a genuine buzz. The survivors were a very determined bunch, and I felt that this might just work out after all.

At my second or third visit to the BL board, reporting back on my survival plan, I could point to the reduced costs and the still-improving quality. All now rested on my sales forecast for the 1982 season. We needed sales of 22,000 cars but BL European and Overseas, or BLEO, the sales offshoot who sold our cars, would not allow me a forecast of more than 18,000, a number which still left us in a loss-making position. The only sales force I could influence was through our common-cause arrangements with the North American sales companies. To make things add up, the first thing was to persuade our US company to raise sales from 3,000 to 9,000 in 1982. Enthusiastic as they were, they could only envisage 6,000, which was included in the forecast. In any event, they were still part of BLEO, and their bosses there had never experienced success – they did not really believe 6,000 sales were possible. We were at an impasse.

I must say that bureaucracy is the most discouraging of all human barriers. I believe I was at my most disheartened. My wife had to encourage me with a drink to get out of the car when I got home. I was battle-weary and the future seemed to hold very few options.

The only step left was to increase the sales forecast – and then deliver on it. The US dealers were the only ones with the dynamism and the horsepower to do this. I had sensed in my meetings the previous year that if I could give them good cars, they would do the rest. They were all independent businessmen, and they had their livelihoods on the line. They could always sell other products: they did not need to sell Jaguars if there was anything better to keep them busy. But they were natural enthusiasts, they were natural believers. Somehow, we had to make them believe even more. I began to form the hunch that my newly-energised, albeit somewhat battered, workforce were the people to do this job.

We created a 'Royal Route' through each of our factories where we would take the dealers when they visited, and I went round explaining to the workforce that now was the time to sell what they could do. They had to sell to the dealers their own belief in their own capabilities – that they knew what they were doing and that they were good at what they did. If they wanted to be in work next year they would have to do this – and do it all very well.

The management team planned this most important American dealer visit, with everybody throwing in their best ideas. I impressed on The Lord Lieutenant of Warwickshire that I wanted him to host a cocktail party, when the dealers arrived, in the historic Shire Hall. They would then be led by a knight on horseback to Warwick Castle. There was a lone piper playing on the battlements. A fine dinner would be arranged in the Great Hall, with minstrels in the gallery.

This all went as planned, and I knew we had it about right when our only complaint from our guests was that they were running out of film. I told the dealers and their wives that on their tours of the factories they must talk to the workforce and make up their own minds as to whether these men and women really were trying to make good cars. They would test-drive the new 1982 cars and we would all meet at the end of the visit to discuss the future.

In his bootlace tie and fancy shirt, nobody in the workforce could doubt that Gene Fisher, our Dallas Fort Worth dealer and chairman of the dealer council, was an American dealer. People were jumping off the tracks and grabbing hold of him, to show him what they did. It was happening all up and down the tracks. There was an exciting, almost tangible feeling of goodwill as workforce and dealers mingled.

Gene came up to me shaking his head and said, 'Well, John, when are you going to take these movie actors away and bring back the real workforce?' At the end of the trip we all gathered in the Stratford-upon-Avon Hilton to take stock. After my speech thanking the dealers for being with us, I asked for questions before I summed up our position.

'How did the workforce enjoy our visit?' was the first question. 'Well, I don't know,' I replied, putting on a perplexed expression. 'The workforce asked much the same question. I said to them, "You know how Americans are – they are much more reserved than we are, and don't tell you what is on their minds..."'

'Well, you must go back and tell them how much we enjoyed the visit,' someone said. 'Couldn't they see that?' I'd dangled my hook. Now it was time to spool them in.

'The problem is this,' I said. 'Their livelihoods are at stake if you don't sell the cars. Right now the sales forecast that you have sent in is for 6,000 cars. But they need 9,000 to keep their jobs.'

There was a hushed sort of sigh. Low whisperings were going on at each of the tables. What was going to happen next? At this point Robbie Robinson, a cockney who had emigrated to the United States, stood up. 'I think that I speak for all the dealers here from Southern California. We will take 50 per cent more cars. From what I have seen today, we can sell these cars. We are not going to let these folks down, and they are not going to let us down.'

With that, the other tables stood up to say that they could sell 50 per cent more, until all were on their feet, shouting, 'Fifty per cent more!'

I quietened the audience and said to Graham Whitehead, 'Well, Graham, what is your forecast for 1982, is it 6,000 or 9,000?'

Graham replied quietly but firmly. 'It's 9,000, Mr Chairman.'

With that, I signalled, and in came the band of the Royal Marines playing 'Land of Hope and Glory'. I have no idea how Graham convinced BLEO that he could sell 9,000 cars. Knowing Graham, he probably told BLEO that he already had all the orders in hand following the dealer visit.

I got the last 1,000 sales required for the forecast partly from an exhausting three-day trip to Australia, where John Shingleton ('Shingo' in Aussie-speak) organised a rerun of my US quality visit. All went well except for the gypsy band playing next door in Brisbane, which threatened to drown out my speech. John Mackie in Canada bravely added more sales to his forecast.

We finally submitted a 22,000 forecast to the BL board for the 1982 model year, and this was accepted. The Jaguar story could continue.

The US, Canadian and Australian sales companies were the only BLEO operations prepared to increase their sales forecasts, thanks to the strong independent initiative we took. It was a close-run thing, as no other BLEO company, including that for the UK, made any effort to do so.

As it turned out, we sold 9,700 cars in the US in 1982 and 22,500 worldwide. We started making a profit in September 1981 and were profitable for the year of 1982. We did not make a loss again.

Chapter 8

The turnaround

1981-82

The great debate we had with the US dealers gave us a sales forecast that required us to double our productivity in order to break even. That job still had to be done. Forecasts are one thing; doing it is another.

Nor will breaking even do for long in the car business. You need new models. For that you need to have engineers to design new cars, and I thought we needed about 1,000 of those, versus the 200 we already had. We needed to invest £100 million per year in new tooling and equipment, against the virtually nothing that we were spending at that time. This all added up, together with financing costs, to about £200 million extra in gross profit being needed just to make us viable. This meant making four cars per employee, not the three we assumed we needed to break even. We needed more sales, but could take on no more employees, apart from engineers. That was the harsh arithmetic of the plan.

At that time the trade union movement had an institutionalised opposition to productivity improvement. The shop stewards had an easy life looking for trouble but doing no work themselves, which clearly made them feel guilty. They expunged this guilt by seeing it as their duty to assist their members to do as little work as possible for the maximum pay. That seemed the full scope of their vision.

I have listened to shop stewards explaining how they taught their members to bamboozle the time-study engineers to allocate excess time to their efforts, whilst still appearing busy. At the very beginning, I might have got the shop stewards to help Jaguar to survive. After all, it was a golden goose to them, and with no goose there would be no golden eggs. But to increase productivity I was going to have to fight a wily enemy; the workforce were going to have to want to do a better job against the advice and wisdom of their shop stewards.

This was going to be a battle of wills and skills. This was not going to be solved the conventional way, with time-study engineers. The process improvements would have to be delegated to the operator – our workforce would have to bring their enthusiasm and brains to work, as well as their hands and feet. To get started we would have to explain to the whole workforce why we would need this radical increase in productivity.

The first weapon we chose was a 'hearts and minds' programme, led by Mike Kinski, our training manager, helped by his brilliant and enthusiastic ally Josie Freedman.

Nothing fazed them, nothing deterred them. We were going to explain why we needed this improvement in productivity in an irresistibly compelling manner. I wanted every employee to attend an evening event with his wife – the wives might be tougher than the shop stewards, I thought. I envisaged a chicken supper with a glass of wine, a presentation of what needed to be done and why, a question-and-answer session, and something to send people away thoughtful but stimulated.

They came back with a dazzling video with the comedienne Pamela Stephenson, a great actress, pretending to be a car being made by our employees and acting out the rough ride she got, as opposed to what she thought was her due. She was extremely colourful in her reaction when badly handled. It was a riot, and extraordinarily innovative.

Every question-and-answer session had to be run by one of the directors. A comedian would then be brought on to 'tidy up', with some thoughts of his own. Hopefully everybody would go home happy and motivated. The company caterers were on pain of death to wine and dine our guests well.

Some of our directors were very good at running these shows. In particular, Pat Audrain, the purchasing director, had star billing – he even gained a following in Japan after a Japanese TV company made a programme of his efforts. His leadership and enthusiasm were extolled as the new way of management.

The 'hearts and minds' operation became a continuous programme of events, including new-car launches, cricket matches and visits to watch our racing cars. We built a swimming pool and a sports centre. Every Jaguar employee could have a Jaguar car and driver for their wedding. Anything that drew the Jaguar family together was considered.

All these programmes were run by senior Jaguar managers who contributed their own expertise and enthusiasm to make them a success. The most prolific contribution was made by George Hind, a senior manufacturing manager, who when told that there was to be no pantomime at the Coventry Theatre, said, 'This has to change – there will be a pantomime for our children!' And so there was.

The second big programme was Open Learning. We had a massive shortage of skills and knowledge. Our idea was to create an open university offering the skills we needed, plus the basic preparatory skills that would enable employees to pursue further education to suit their own career choices. At that time only about eight or nine per cent of adults went to university, and Jaguar needed far more than that percentage in order to be internationally competitive.

We went into joint ventures with local schools, further education colleges and universities. At first, we offered only training in the skills we needed right away, and the classroom was in our Computer-Assisted Learning Centre. The courses included computer and keyboard skills, statistical process control, mathematics, critical-path planning, production and inventory control, and – importantly – the German language. The view in Germany now was that we might remain in business long enough to be worth supplying, and so we needed to be able to talk to our best suppliers in their own language.

Employees, with permission from their boss, could pursue these courses in company time, or in their own time if they wished. Eventually these courses were extended to include general education. Mike Kinski, together with George Bain, then Dean of Warwick Business School, created the country's first part-time MBA course and Mike was the first graduate.

Our general concept was that you joined Jaguar to get on in life and, no matter what level of education you joined with, we would help you to go as far as you could go or wanted to go. We thought this outbid the shop stewards' notion of maximum pay for minimum effort, at least for many of our employees. Eventually over 40 per cent of the workforce took part in these learning programmes.

But the heavy lifting would have to be done by the foremen and team leaders on the shopfloor, with their quality circles of employees, and with the emphasis now moving on from 'right first time' quality to process improvement, with quality as the driver. It was done with varying levels of capability and enthusiasm, and management was very much in a helping mode, to fill in the gaps. We all bustled around looking for things that would help the team leaders to make the improvements; if something worked in one place, we would peddle it to other groups. We looked for bottlenecks we could clear, constantly searching out those needing help. Huge strides were made in the logistics of getting parts to the tracks.

These process improvements were the key, and between 1980 and 1984 there was a steady reduction in the man-hours per XJ6 from a virtually hand-built 700 hours per car down to 300 hours. Productivity improved by getting things right first time and thus eliminating reworking, but more than anything else, better processes gave a much more statistical control of variability. The improved quality triggered the Quality Index to start paying bonuses as soon as the volume increased.

Everyone was now a winner: customers were getting better cars, the employees were getting bonuses, and Jaguar was making the profits needed to start funding the new model programme. Across a two-year period our productivity almost trebled.

We already had awards schemes for quality and process improvements, but the US dealers added their own awards on top. Every month a thousand dollars was given to the three best process improvements that in the dealers' judgement made a difference to the customer. There was tremendous motivation generated by these awards, with the dealers giving them directly to the employees. Receiving one of these dealer awards was a source of great pride.

Many of the most troublesome shop stewards had left when we had our voluntary redundancy programme. However, in our fight to become successful, I hated the idea that those remaining might be plotting full-time for our downfall. I therefore insisted that all were assigned duties. I was under no illusion that these duties would be done well, but at least it would complicate their lives: they were the enemy, and they could still kill the company if we allowed them to do so.

They demonstrated that they were not subdued, for at each of the 1981 and 1982 wage rounds we had strikes in pursuit of wage demands. Jaguar's terms and conditions were the same as in the rest of BL and Michael

Edwardes was setting the terms of the annual increases; they certainly were not generous but were the absolute limit of what BL could afford. The Thatcher Government hated subsidising people who would not try to help themselves.

As time went on, we could see that a 300 per cent or even 400 per cent increase in productivity at Jaguar was feasible, so Jaguar could have financed a higher increase than the other BL companies. But quite rightly, Michael held my feet to the fire with the rest and so we had strikes along with all the other companies.

But I was always searching for a solution. If Michael's shoot-out with the unions failed, and led to the closure of BL Cars, maybe that would be the time for me and the management to buy Jaguar for a reasonable sum. There would be no other takers, for nobody else could even guess at our rapidly increasing viability. In both years I explored the possibilities, and I could have gained the funding. In 1981 we would only have needed working capital, and Brian Pitman, the general manager of Lloyds Bank, would have supported us. In 1982, when we might have needed £50 million or £100 million more, Ian MacGregor of Lazards was also supportive. I was not going to let the possible bankruptcy of BL slow us down.

But in both years, with steely determination, Michael made the unions back down. When he had made his final offer, that was his final offer. Grand speeches, long hours at ACAS, the Government's arbitration service, and strikes, anger and all the stock-in-trade of the unions made no difference. The final offer was the final offer.

These wage negotiations developed into enthralling acts of theatre. We made an offer which was usually all that was possible if BL were to remain viable; this offer was always rejected by the unions as derisory. A tiny increase would then be conceded in negotiation and a final offer made to

---

Not only did we enjoy the backing of Norman Tebbit but the Prime Minister, Margaret Thatcher, was also an enthusiastic supporter and created the industrial environment in which we wrested back control from the unions and could succeed. (The Observer/Rex Features)

Bob Tullius's Group 44 team boosted the XJ-S's image and sales in the USA by winning the 1978 Trans-Am Championship. I was very aware that racing was important to Jaguar. (Jaguar North America)

the workers which would then be rejected at angry mass meetings.

The strikes would start, at which point Michael Edwardes and we, his managers, would meet the unions at ACAS for the process of arbitration. The unions would always be angry and bitter, with occasional noisy demonstrations outside, for the benefit of the TV cameras.

ACAS officials would scurry between the two parties for a number of hours; occasionally, concessions unrelated to pay might be made in corridor negotiations, and finally, after 12 hours or so, the first face-to-face meeting would occur between BL's personnel director, Geoff Armstrong, and the union lead negotiator. Geoff would patiently explain that there was no more money to give, and the union leader would ask for a modest concession, which we would reject.

Eventually, after many more hours, an even smaller concession would be asked for by the unions, at which point Michael would gather us together to see who wanted to concede. In particular, he would encourage me to say if I could afford it. Michael always seemed to enjoy these very tense situations. But we would all reject the concession and Michael himself would tell the gathered union delegates that there was no more money and, if they stayed out on strike, he would declare BL bankrupt.

The unions then had to decide whether or not to call his bluff. One thing they did know was that appeals to the Prime Minister would not lead to beer and sandwiches and giving in: they would go unheard. Margaret Thatcher did not do that sort of thing. They always backed down and accepted.

I remember thinking at the time that if Lord Stokes had tried to be brave and behave in a similar manner to Michael Edwardes, no Labour Prime Minister, whether Harold Wilson or Jim Callaghan, would have backed him up. Perhaps that is why he held back. How restless would his shareholders have become? They would have been absolutely terrified if they had learned what 'Red Robbo' and his henchmen looked like, and understood that they were the ones really in charge of the shop floor, and hence the company.

One person who had noticed Jaguar's improvements in quality and reliability was Eberhard von Kuenheim, the chairman of BMW. He was doing similar JD Power surveys to ours. He had gained permission from the BL board to discuss a possible long-term relationship with us at Jaguar. In planning his visit, I arranged for Jaguar's chauffeur, Don Currie, to meet him at Birmingham Airport's private aviation terminal.

Don had fought with the Eighth Army from El Alamein and up into Italy, and he seemed pretty uncomfortable with his assignment, especially when I reinforced the instruction that he had to be especially welcoming to our German guest. He said, 'Should I wear my medals, Sir?' When I asked why, he replied, 'I'm not sure I know how to be nice to Germans, but they might appreciate my medals,' and then added, 'I've shot a few, mind.' However, I need not have been afraid: they were firm friends by the time I welcomed Dr von Kuenheim to Browns Lane.

As mentioned earlier, von Kuenheim had been very helpful to me when I had started at Jaguar, by encouraging his engineers to solve one or two of my own quality issues. He was a courteous and interested guest, impressed by our progress and anxious to explore some sort of tie-up, even a possible purchase of Jaguar. At that time I just wanted to run with the ball as far down the field as we could go. I had no idea how far that would be, nor did I perceive that we would need a place of greater safety than being on our own.

I was not therefore very encouraging. I said that if he pursued his proposal he must not assume that the Jaguar management would go with the company if he bought it. He laughed and said that he was too nervous of car-building in the UK to buy Jaguar without its management.

We parted on good terms – at least our efforts had received an accolade from one of the titans of the industry. I was always grateful for the help and encouragement von Kuenheim had given us. However, I turned down the idea of a relationship with BMW, because I felt they would restrict us to the luxury sector and inhibit our expansion into the very lucrative executive market that we had legendarily exploited with the Mk 2.

As soon as Jaguar had turned the corner and was making small profits, the responsibility for the North American companies was transferred to Jaguar. The president, Graham Whitehead, and the sales and marketing vice-president, Mike Dale, were already a formidable team. They had sensibly reduced the dealer network to only those who were capable of giving customer service; all of the US senior management had spent many hours in courts to achieve this. Now we could make our contribution. We did a retro-fit of troublesome components on cars built before the 1982 model year.

To get our sales of the 1982 models off to a good start, we had also reduced prices and now the cars were very competitively priced. We picked our own niche above the US competition but below our German rivals. All of this had gone down very well with the motoring press.

Each month I chaired the Jaguar North America board meeting and then spent two days or so with the dealers. I was struck by their energy, enthusiasm and inventiveness. No two seemed to go about their task in the same way and our programmes were designed to support their considerable and varied efforts.

In the major cities we ran pooled dealer advertising to get the customers into the dealerships, and test-drive what were almost new vehicles to the market place. Typically, I would meet the local press, who were extremely interested in our 'Man bites dog' story. Here was a British car manufacturer doing well, and profitably selling cars which satisfied customers in the United States.

In the evening we would have a party for customers who were interested in this strange story of a successful car company emerging out of strike-prone England. Jaguar began to generate momentum, success generated its own further success. Together we were all putting legend back into the Jaguar Legend Bank.

I never ceased to be amazed at the entrepreneurial flair of the dealers. One dealer simply used the Internal Revenue Services tax records to contact everyone in his district earning more than $100,000, and tried different ways of tempting them to take a test drive: a bottle of champagne, smoked salmon, theatre tickets, sending a test car to their home or driving them to work... anything that got them into a Jaguar.

Another one used the customer traffic flow brought in by our shared dealer advertising. With a huge stock of ready-to-sell cars, he would ask the customer what colour and specification would be his, or more usually her, dream car. After showing the customer round the dealership he would take them to the 'delivery room' and there, through the mists of dry ice, and with a glass of champagne in their hand, they would see the car of their dreams. They had an unbelievably high conversion rate – but then it was a very beautiful car.

A third dealer simply cherished his customers. He was the one, who in our darkest days, used to follow his new customers home to make sure they got there. Nothing was too much trouble: whatever the question, the answer was 'Yes'.

I was also intrigued by the way the dealers used the Bob Tullius Group 44 XJ-S racing programme. This quite successful team, sponsored by Jaguar US and the Quaker State oil company, was winning a lot of friends. Wherever they raced, the local dealers would bring along their customers, give them lunch, and then they would watch the race. Win or lose, everybody enjoyed the day as long as we were competitive – and especially when we won, which of course helped underscore our story of increased reliability. I stored this up as a useful idea for when we had our own sales operation in Europe.

We could see from our North American experience that we now had eminently saleable cars, sold by an excellent team and very capable dealers, but elsewhere very little was happening. We had been given our own first-rate PR director, David Boole, and a very able liaison director, Neil Johnson, to encourage focus on Jaguar in BLEO, the unwieldy and mostly moribund BL sales operation.

Neil was frustrated by having to deal with a sales network where the Jaguar franchise had been given to every BL dealer who wanted it. In particular, the BL dealer body in the UK was dominated by the huge groups of volume-car dealers, often with 50 or so outlets, perhaps 10 of which might be selling Jaguars. Most of the old Jaguar outlets had been family-run, with only one dealership, and in the main they had been forced out by BLEO. Of course these traditional dealers not only knew their customers personally, but also gave impeccable service – much like the better dealers in the US.

In a quite shameless and brutal fashion, I agitated with senior BL management to hand over to Neil the actual running of at least the UK network. After much infighting, this was done.

He in turn hired the highly-regarded sales and marketing director of Lotus, Roger Putnam. But before these two could get on with selling cars, they had to cull the bad dealers, encourage the good ones to give better service with a minimum-standards programme, and find some new dealers in key areas. We were planning to cut 300 outlets down to about 100 or so. This surgery was of course only possible because our sales targets were already being met by the growth of the US market. We could thus afford the odd hiccup as we lost some dealers and put new ones in place. Roger and his sales team embarked on an extremely robust campaign to reduce the bloated UK sales network.

The cull was announced at our first home-grown dealer meeting. We began by announcing the minimum-standards programme, which included a new corporate identity, a stylish but very British décor, and minimum servicing standards. There was a sharp intake of breath. Many of the dealers were losing money on the franchise and now there was this extra expense. I played hard-ball.

'I would like you to introduce yourself to the dealer on your left, and now to the one on your right,' I said. 'Next time we meet, I want you all to understand only one of you three will still be with us.' We then went on to describe all we were going to do to help them sell. They were already reading in the national newspapers of the success we were having with quality and productivity, the growing success we were having in the US, and how well the 1982 cars were being reviewed by the motoring pundits.

David Boole, our new PR man, had started a process of having our cars reappraised by the UK motoring press and we were now getting similar rave reviews to those in the US press. The 1982 XJ12 HE was rated 'the best car in the world' by one magazine. David also outlined a series of Jaguar evenings that he wanted the dealers to run, at which they could display the new corporate identity to their customers and a Jaguar director would be there to describe our extraordinary improvements in quality and manufacturing efficiency.

During 1982 we indeed reduced our UK dealers from 300 to approaching 100 and increased sales by 20 per cent – thereby increasing sales per dealer from less than 20 cars to more than 65 cars. The franchise now meant something and the dealers began to be profitable. Now they would really want to try.

One of the traits of leadership that I was picking up from Michael Edwardes was to be willing to take on the most difficult tasks and not, as boss, take the soft option. When one of the major dealers with 10 of our

I headhunted Roger Putnam (top left) from Lotus, where he was sales & marketing director, to fulfil the same role for us. He would transform the dealer network. Roger originally worked for Neil Johnson (top right) before Neil was seconded to the Ministry of Defence and took command of the 4th Battalion The Royal Green Jackets. (Philip Porter Archive)

We regularly illustrated our sales performance in Topics, *the in-house magazine for employees. (Philip Porter Archive)*

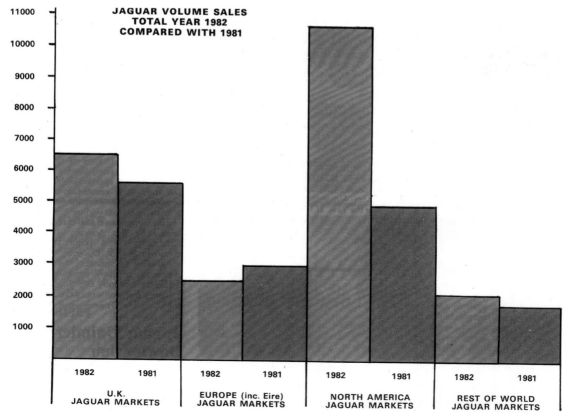

JAGUAR VOLUME SALES
TOTAL YEAR 1982
COMPARED WITH 1981

11000		
10000		
9000		
8000		
7000		
6000		
5000		
4000		
3000		
2000		
1000		

1982	1981	1982	1981	1982	1981	1982	1981
U.K. JAGUAR MARKETS		EUROPE (inc. Eire) JAGUAR MARKETS		NORTH AMERICA JAGUAR MARKETS		REST OF WORLD JAGUAR MARKETS	

franchises refused to implement any of our minimum standards, its MD insisted on visiting me to tell me this in person. He said he had a legal contract with BL that did not include any of these minimum standards. At this time, BL only gave their dealers one-year contracts. It was our intention, as part of our package, to give longer contracts – but only if dealers achieved our targets for customer satisfaction.

On this occasion the existing arrangement played into my hands. When he had finished, I said, 'Well, that's fine.' He asked me, 'What do you mean by, "That's fine?"'

I continued, 'When do those contracts terminate?'

'At the end of September,' he replied.

'That's easy, then. We will terminate all your contracts in September, then we'll both be happy,' I told him.

'Not so fast – maybe we should negotiate,' he went on.

'I think that is what we have just done,' I concluded.

Roger Putnam reduced the dominance of major groups in the UK network in similarly robust fashion.

By 1982 we were profitable, but as yet not quite viable in terms of having the financial muscle to fund the new models we so badly needed. Then out of the blue in 1983 the US cavalry came to the rescue, in the shape of the now mighty US dollar exchange rate falling from over $2 to the pound to $1.50 to the pound. For Jaguar this was Christmas Day, Thanksgiving and New Year's Day all rolled into one. The increase in the dollar all went into profit. In three years we had gone from losing £50 million to being able to forecast a £50 million profit in 1983, thanks to all our efforts and now this currency movement.

We were now on our way. We were satisfying our customers, our factories were increasingly productive and our workforce was learning its trade. With this more favourable dollar exchange rate, together with a little more of a productivity increase, we would be able to fund those new models.

We were even winning races again, with a victory in the 1982 Tourist Trophy race. Despite the fact that we were still fighting for our survival, we had seen the long-term marketing advantages of having a successful racing programme. This was a brave decision, in the circumstances, but in late 1981 I had been won over by the persuasiveness of a quite extraordinary man, Tom Walkinshaw, who convinced me that together we could run a team of racing XJ-S coupés.

As we had no money, I had given Tom the incentive of paying him by results. It turned out to be a most satisfactory way forward, and getting Jaguar back into motor sport had a very encouraging impact on us all.

What next?

Chapter 9

Dilemma

1983

The testing programme for the new 3.6-litre AJ6 engine had started well. We had decided not to launch it in the XJ40, but rather to fit it ahead of time to a lightly revised XJ-S. With manual transmission available, the new six-cylinder XJ-S would provide a more economical and more sporting alternative to the automatic-only V12 model. To maximise publicity, the engine was announced at the same time as a very pretty new variant of the XJ-S, the Cabriolet.

We had been mindful of recent US legislation discouraging convertibles, and the enormous engineering load required to design a full convertible. So we limited ourselves to having a rigid roof structure with removable roof panels for the driver and passenger and a folding hood at the back. It was a little unusual, which is why we called it a cabriolet, although we were not quite sure what that meant. But it was a very attractive car, with the torsional stiffness and refinement of the original coupé.

Equally important, it tested the power unit for the future XJ40, meaning that we could get rid of any bugs before using the engine in our crucial new saloon.

We launched the car in what was the traditional Jaguar way. We made a few, in any way we could, allowed our resourceful Press Car team led by Peter Taylor to prepare them for testing by the press, duly received rave reviews, and then in poured the orders – after which we handed the car over to Manufacturing. At this point the fun really started. At any volume above two or three cars per day the engines were so terribly rough and unrefined that they had to be virtually hand-finished.

The journalists who had given us such kind reviews were soon wondering why so few cabriolets were on the road. David Boole, in one of his usual flashes of PR genius, blamed the roof configuration. It was hand-made, as we had not originally intended to make very many, he told the press. We would now put in proper manufacturing facilities, he said, because we were overwhelmed by demand – which was always a good excuse, even with tongue in cheek.

We could not afford a similar débâcle with the XJ40. We would be dead and buried if we had to fully test our manufacturing processes after launch. Engineering had not created a vehicle ready to launch. Right from the time of Sir William Lyons, they had always prided themselves on getting by on a shoestring. This was a perilously dangerous strategy, and one that had to change.

We redoubled our efforts to hire the best engineers we could find, and together with Dave Szczupak, one of our most talented young engineers, I took charge of the AJ6 engine refinement task-force.

The first thing we discovered was that a straight-six aluminium engine was about the most difficult configuration to refine. We would need far more sophisticated engine mountings and extraordinary refinement in tolerances and balance, far beyond anything required by our good-tempered giant of an aluminium V12 engine. We had a lot to learn. We were babies when it came to designing and developing new product. Still, when it came to trouble-shooting, we were ace performers, and after much effort and embarrassment, our Cabriolet eventually became a success.

One of the experimental colours we had tried on one of the cars had been a rich gold which matched my wife's blonde hair, and I was at last a star when I took it home for her 40th birthday.

As a further result of our experiences with the Cabriolet and its engine, I began chairing the XJ40 launch programme, and grew increasingly gloomy. This car was not going to be ready to launch the next year, nor were we in a position to make it ready to launch, try as we might. In my personal opinion it was not yet as good as the XJ6 that it was intended to replace.

Unfortunately for us, Michael Edwardes had left BL to return to Chloride and rational decision-making was leaving with him. I realised that to keep my job I would have to launch the XJ40, ready or not. That was the macho spirit engendered by the new management of BL Cars under Ray Horrocks.

Alarmingly, BL had commissioned a review by distinguished academic engineer Bob Lickley, to determine whether XJ40 would be ready for production in the autumn of 1984. After painstakingly reviewing all elements of the programme, he had concluded that, 'Full engineering sign-off by June 1984 and production by autumn should be achieved.'

I was not persuaded. I wanted 200 pre-production cars made by Manufacturing and 100,000 miles of testing under our belt before I would be convinced. I was mindful that BL Cars, and BLMC before them, had never launched a world-class car, tough and refined enough to be sold anywhere. A Jaguar could not be anything less than world-class.

Meanwhile there were political pressures entering the picture. The Thatcher Government was publicly agitating that as a price for further investment in BL the company must show willing, and create some of its own capital by selling something. The BL position under Michael Edwardes was that the company as a whole should be privatised. It was felt that if the 'Crown Jewels' were sold off piecemeal as they achieved viability, this would weaken and demoralise the ever-diminishing rump that was left. This was a perfectly reasonable position.

In early 1983 there was only one viable company, Land Rover, which rather bizarrely was part of the BL Truck and Bus Division, and was the only part of that division which was profitable. Thus nobody wanted to sell Land Rover, and in any event its performance was deteriorating. Michael Edwardes had been extremely tough and difficult to shift when he had made up his mind. Maybe the new board under the chairmanship of Sir Austin Bide could be hustled into a different position? These were uncertainties that were creating dilemmas for everyone.

Back in the real world, Jaguar was booming. We were easily going to meet our forecast of 28,000 cars for 1983 and we were now forecasting

The XJ-S Cabriolet was a happy compromise between the Coupé, with its controversial 'flying buttresses', and a full convertible. We also introduced the more economical AJ6 engine with this model. (Philip Porter Archive)

Before launching the XJ6 replacement, code-named the XJ40, we were determined to carry out considerable testing, including in hotter climates. (Philip Porter Archive)

more than 32,000 for 1984, which for Jaguar might turn into an all-time record. The XJ-S, which had been selling so poorly that its continued production had looked threatened, was now a success, thanks to its revised HE engine. So we now had two product lines, not just one.

Productivity continued to increase and quality to improve. The dollar remained at around $1.50 to the pound, and we now anticipated profits for 1984 of almost £100 million – about what I thought we needed to become a viable independent company. I decided to go back on the trail of completing the piecing together of the company. We gained responsibility for systems development, pushing forward a huge computer-aided design (CAD) programme for engineering, and we gained a treasury operation where we began studying the operation of a dollar/pound currency-hedging programme.

We had demonstrated conclusively to ourselves that we were better at selling cars than BLEO and started examining how to sell into our third-largest market, Germany, which was also by now a very big supplier of components. Better than hedging our purchasing of Deutschmarks, we thought, let's sell cars to balance the books.

The TWR racing programme was also continuing to be a success. I had been present when we had beaten BMW into second place at Donington, with a very young Martin Brundle driving the XJ-S brilliantly in very wet conditions. As Neil Johnson and I walked past the BMW pits, they complained that we had used some unfair tactics. 'This is not World War Two,' they shouted. 'No, but the result was the same,' Neil shouted in reply. The whole company seemed to be firing on all twelve cylinders.

During the year we had a large number of Cabinet members come to see us: Geoffrey Howe, the Chancellor, Norman Tebbit, our saviour when Secretary of State for Industry and whom we discovered had once been a Jaguar XK 150 owner, and Cecil Parkinson, the rising star of the Tory party. They were all rejoicing at the Jaguar story happening on their watch, knowing that without their efforts we would not have existed at all, never mind been successful.

I wondered at the time, all the same, whether they were looking over the company for some other purpose, rather than just preening their political feathers.

Then, out of the blue came the news that General Motors was interested in buying Jaguar and had for some time been in discussions with Ray

Horrocks, the chief executive of BL Cars, and members of Central Staff. The American giant would like to move the discussions on by coming to see Jaguar, 'kicking the tyres' and meeting the management. In our early discussions, I made my own personal position clear. Depending on the nature of the interest, I would not necessarily go with the company if GM bought it, and in any event I would want to hear about any future relationship from Roger Smith, the GM chairman.

I knew from my previous life with GM that you had to go to the top if you wanted a vision that lasted longer than the 12-month budget.

Ray Horrocks and I had those discussions with Roger Smith and his colleagues a few weeks later in Detroit. Roger was extremely courteous and thoughtful, and said that he regarded the meeting as exploration to try to find a best fit. He mused that he could not sell an automobile for more than $20,000. Jaguar could and, what is more, GM products sold alongside Jaguars would gain prestige from being sold that way. He was willing to let Jaguar remain somewhat independent, he said, but the more ownership GM had, the more help it would be able to give Jaguar.

On the other hand, he did point out that a company like ours was very vulnerable if we ever produced a less-than-excellent new model. GM could then be a safe port in a storm. Ray Horrocks left Detroit uncommitted, but expressing a willingness to give Roger's ideas earnest consideration.

I was not convinced. Outside their core North American business, which was meticulously honed by years of practice, US car companies tended to be short-term and haphazard in their management. Unprofitable orphans would be cast off in a storm, not nursed back to health.

I concluded that it was better to go for independence and then see what happened. General Motors made it clear that they were willing to buy Jaguar when they contacted Norman Lamont, then the Chief Secretary to the Treasury, after he had publicly reiterated that the Government expected the BL board to start a privatisation programme, as a condition of any further Government aid.

Another Chinese-style crisis-cum-opportunity was clearly looming – and the danger was that we were not safe with BL any longer. Not only might we have to launch XJ40 before it was ready, but BL itself might have to sell us to an unsuitable bidder if it lost the argument with the Government.

Could the opportunity part of the equation be that we privatise Jaguar ourselves?

I offered to lead a management buy-out. This was met with shock and horror by BL. Clearly, it was rather primly pointed out, I would have to resign if I wished to do anything so outrageous. It might bring profit to me personally, and that would never do. Resigning was a most unattractive proposition. What would they do with the business whilst my back was turned? It was very different from doing business with Michael. With him you could have a grown-up conversation and fairly quickly work out a mutually-satisfactory plan of campaign. Now it was more a case of suggest-and-duck.

It was into this turmoil of much risk with very little opportunity that I received a telephone call from Norman Lamont himself. Could we meet in confidence, and in some secrecy, to discuss possible future scenarios for Jaguar's future?

We would meet for lunch in the basement restaurant of the Tate Gallery and I should ask for 'Mr Norman'. I arrived early, as I always do for appointments, but at the Tate I could at least revisit one of my thinking haunts from when I had been a student at Imperial College. I wandered around, absent-mindedly looking at the French Impressionists, wondering what my sticking points should be, in what I assumed would be some sort of deal. I concluded that the core concept was finding a safer home than BL. After that, everything was negotiable.

Norman was on time, which I later discovered to be unusual for politicians. He also allowed all the options to be thoughtfully and carefully considered, which was more than I got from my BL management. 'As you know, we could force BL to sell Jaguar, and GM does seem to be willing to buy,' he started.

'GM has enough companies in the UK that are losing money, and I have made it clear that the management does not necessarily go with the

---

Our new, all-aluminium AJ6 six-cylinder engine would replace the old faithful XK power unit which had been first introduced in 1948 and sustained the company since then. The AJ6 was not without its problems initially. (Jon Pressnell Collection)

I was very happy to take advice from, and discussed many matters with, Sir William Lyons. It was, after all, 'his' company, having founded it with a partner in 1922. (Philip Porter Archive)

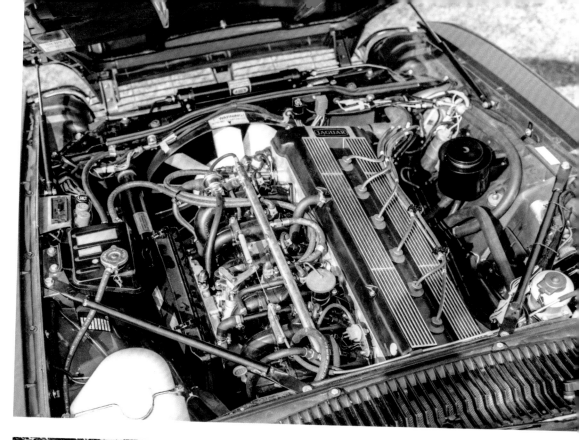

company, so such an option is not without controversy,' I replied.

He asked what my preferred option might be. 'We should go for independence,' I said. 'It will be quite some time before we would be strong enough to fight off predators, so we should be a private company. I know that we could raise the money for a management buy-out now, but if we delay too long it will become very expensive. Our performance is improving very rapidly and we have an attractive dollar exchange rate.'

I thought being candid was the right thing to be, but Norman was not convinced by my argument. 'That is not an attractive solution for the Government,' he replied. 'We have the monster privatisation of British Telecom in late 1984, and a successful privatisation of Jaguar earlier would set the right tone. Getting BT right is worth billions to the Treasury. But BT will have a Golden Share, so why not Jaguar?'

Being a sprat to catch a mackerel did not particularly appeal to me, but the Golden Share did. The Golden Share was an exquisite device, as the consent of whomsoever held it – in this case the Government – would be required in order for ownership of the company to change. I asked for how long the Golden Share would be in place. 'What we are doing today is creating an envelope of opportunity, and that will include an Initial Public Offering, possibly a Golden Share, and it will have to be soon,' he summarised. 'But it won't include a buy-out by the management.' I gave Lamont my reaction.

'I will discuss all of this with my management, but we will need a Golden Share. Without that, an IPO will just be the start of a bidding war.' He brought the discussion to a close.

'Ring me tomorrow,' he said. 'Let me know the reply and I will let you know about the Golden Share.'

Later that evening I gathered the management team together and described Norman Lamont's 'envelope of opportunity'. I pointed out that it had all been discussed calmly and rationally and that in my opinion Lamont seemed entirely confident of delivering it all. He seemed to be speaking for the Cabinet as a whole. To a man my team all concluded that floating the company was safer than staying where we were; even the Golden Share was negotiable. Staying where we were was full of peril.

I had arranged to meet Bill Lyons that night. I not only saw it as a courtesy to discuss big events with him, but he always had very clear insights into our situation. After he had busied himself getting us some sherry, I asked him what he thought of our famous 'envelope of opportunity'.

We had a long and thoughtful discussion. He was worried about independence. He had rejected the idea when he had realised he had no-one he could leave in charge to carry on the business after he retired. As mentioned previously, he had also been concerned when Pressed Steel, which made his bodies, had been bought by BMC.

I mentioned Roger Smith's thoughts about what might happen if a new model failed, but he smiled and said that you could always muddle through, especially if you took great care and had not spent too much on development. He never did, he pointed out. He reassured me that the XJ40 was a Jaguar, but there were still some visual details he wanted to improve.

He was more supportive of the buy-out option, but if that were not possible, then he too would support an IPO.

I had always assumed that it had been the risks of launching a new model – in this instance the original XJ6 – that had caused him to sell his business. My take on our discussion was that I should not be spooked by launching XJ40, but that I should take great care about getting it right. I gritted my teeth and decided that XJ40 was my priority, even if that meant delaying the launch, and that an IPO was a good way to delay it. That is what we would do.

I rang Norman Lamont the following day, and he told me we could have a Golden Share for five years. I told him we would receive an IPO plan enthusiastically. With that, he told me to deny that any discussions had taken place, to put my hard hat on, and await events.

Chapter 10

Privatisation

1984

We had been pursuing a privatisation checklist for some time, but with little urgency, through our Jaguar Holdings board, chaired by my boss Ray Horrocks. The current timetable required us to launch XJ40 in autumn 1984, and privatise thereafter. This would enable BL Cars to have the enhanced value gained from a successful launch. Following my conversation with Norman Lamont, John Edwards and I reviewed the privatisation checklist in order to speed things up, as we might now need it sooner rather than later.

We had numerous contracts to agree with our colleagues in the rest of BL. Amongst these was that for the design and supply of pressed steel panels – which they did very badly, so any contract would need to be for as short a period as possible, whilst we looked for an alternative supplier. BL also did a poor job selling our cars in Europe and overseas, so we would want to give 12 months' notice of termination of the contract with BLEO. Distribution of replacement parts to our dealers worldwide was done well by Unipart, and would continue in the same way. I knew from my previous experience with Unipart that Jaguar had actually lost money on this when it had done it for itself.

John Edwards had an immense workload on the accounting side, as he had to create a notional five-year trading history and prepare a Stock Exchange prospectus. Amongst the endless lists of things we had to deal with was one potential showstopper: we did not own the Jaguar name. BL had allowed ownership to lapse following the Ryder Report and the subsequent amalgamation of all the marques into BL. The name was owned, in the Commonwealth at least, by a company in Pakistan making low-priced tennis and other racquets.

We had given the task of solving this problem to John Morgan, Jaguar's European liaison director and a truly inventive 'Mr Fixit'. The owner did not want to sell the name but he would sell the company, for a very modest price, if he could stay and run it. John liked the owner and he thought he might be a very good businessman. He was also intrigued by the potential offered by the situation. Why not go up-market with these 'Jaguar' racquets and introduce other products that our dealers could sell?

The Pakistanis already had a smart sports bag in British Racing Green with a leaping Jaguar logo imprinted in gold. So we bought the company, and the sports bag eventually became the leading sports bag in the UK. That company turned out to be a profitable purchase.

The BL board began formulating our future in what turned out to be a process full of potential body-blows to Jaguar, but we were helped by manipulation behind the scenes by Norman Lamont and Margaret Thatcher's Cabinet.

The BL board ruled out selling to General Motors and they moved Jaguar ahead of Land Rover in the queue to privatise. But they left the timing of the float versus the XJ40 launch in the air. Supported by the Department of Trade and Industry, they also proposed to keep a 25 per cent stake in Jaguar. However, in view of BL's very poor performance under our internal contracts, we were opposed to this on the basis that it constituted a potential interference in our affairs – and quite possibly an attempt to exert control over us.

I had decided when I joined Jaguar that my loyalties were to Jaguar itself and its long-term health. Now that we had lost our protecting hand with the departure of Michael Edwardes, I felt little loyalty to BL itself. I thus started to try to improve our bargaining position through my contact with Norman Lamont, and I passed my concerns through to him.

At about this point Ray Horrocks, John Edwards and I had one of our last decent conversations together. I pointed out that we were still a very small company. My line was that we could only do one thing at a time and if we launched the XJ40 first, we would have to ignore privatisation completely – and I knew how impatient the Government was becoming. We would much prefer to privatise, which was relatively easy, and when that was done and dusted we could put all our energies into the much more difficult task of launching the new car.

Ray was thoughtful and promised to think about the timing. John and I thought it was best to get this out of the way before we tackled the 25 per cent ownership issue. We went down to the next planning meeting with BL's advisers, Hill Samuel, still uncertain as to how and when the privatisation process would actually begin. We were sworn to secrecy by Hill Samuel, but were confidentially told, in whispers, that they were planning on an early privatisation, and that BL would retain 25 per cent.

On TV that very night, there was a news item that Jaguar was to be 75 per cent floated and that GM was interested in buying the whole company. This was one of my earliest experiences of 'confidential' Government briefings hustling a situation.

It was rumoured that the final decision, all the same, would be made by Margaret Thatcher herself. Within days, BL was instructed to float 100 per cent of Jaguar and do it straight away. The launch of the XJ40 would have to wait.

We had won that one, and were deeply relieved.

John Edwards and I now entered the maelstrom of expensive activity carried out by investment banks in pursuit of an IPO. We were innocents. Our frugal Northern upbringings were affronted by the sheer extravagance of it all. Vast hordes of bankers, earning the salaries of princes, earnestly tackled the minutiae, appointing advisers here and there whenever an issue threatened to slow them down. The midnight oil was furiously burnt; there were rooms full of warriors in shirt sleeves and braces, earnestly talking on phones, and urgent meetings instantly forming.

Legions of lawyers were appointed, to do the real work of putting ink on the page, and did most of the travelling. They seemed quite inexpensive

---

Top left: Ray Horrocks was for a time chief executive of BL Cars and when Jaguar was privatised became a non-exec director. (LAT)

Top right: The multi-lingual John Morgan was for many years Jaguar export director and did a superb job for the company.

As it says on the cover, this is the Offer for Sale document prepared for the float in 1984. (Philip Porter Archive)

We decided to enter the IMSA sports racing car category in the USA and entrusted this to Group 44 who built the XJR-5 in 1983.

Offer for Sale
by
Hill Samuel & Co. Limited
on behalf of
BLMC Limited

when compared to the investment bankers. On top of the huge expense of creating the prospectus, for which they were extravagantly rewarded, Hill Samuel had the extremely lucrative task of leading the underwriting of the IPO. This task turned out, as we shall see, not to be too onerous. At the end of the food chain were the accountants, whose bills were relatively modest.

In all this, Trevor Swete, the Hill Samuel man in charge, did perform a very useful role as the intermediary between BL Cars and Jaguar management. Without him and his polished diplomacy, I am sure we would have fallen out with each other in a very harmful way. That said, Hill Samuel did impose some very troubling conditions on Jaguar, and the way its board operated. For me the biggest problem was that I had to have a non-executive chairman leading the company in harness with me.

What did a non-executive chairman do? In 1984 they were quite rare beasts and much uncertainty existed as to their duties and responsibilities. I began to feel bad vibrations on this one. I sensed that the years of struggle at Jaguar might have made me very difficult to deal with, and we were far too small a company to have divisions at the top. And what kind of chairman would I have thrust upon me? Would I have any say in the matter – and if so, how would I make the right choice?

I tackled the duties first, and fortuitously met Adrian Cadbury at a Confederation of British Industry seminar. He was the leading proponent of better governance for British boards of directors and was a big supporter of the dual-leadership system. He put it to me very succinctly. It was the job of the chief executive to lead the company. It was the job of the chairman to lead the board. Between them, the two would have a shared view of the policies and strategy of the company.

That seemed all very clear, but how did it work in practice? One of the very few chief executives in the FTSE 100 with a non-executive chairman and whom I knew well enough to ask was Arnold Weinstock of GEC. I rang him up to ask. He seemed very interested and more than helpful when I asked him what a chief executive did and what the non-executive chairman did.

'Why not come to our next GEC board lunch, ask me the question, which I will answer, and we can then all discuss it together,' he said. Well, that was a good offer, and so it happened. I put the question to Arnold and his board colleagues all leant forward. 'Yes, we'd all like to hear this one,' they seemed to murmur in unison.

'It is the job of the chief executive to be a complete dictator,' said Arnold, peering round for added emphasis. 'And in the event that he turns into Napoleon Bonaparte, it is the job of the chairman to shoot him.'

That seemed to be the end of that. There was a little further discussion, much laughter, and it brought the lunch to an end. However, one of the directors later quietly pointed out to me that Arnold had never allowed a chairman to be appointed who would have dared to shoot him.

My investigation came to an end when I went to see a pair I will not name. They professed to work very closely together in much the way Adrian Cadbury recommended. All was sweetness and light, until a few weeks after our meeting I noticed that the chairman had been fired and both duties taken up by the chief executive.

I was by now alarmed enough to recognise that I had to take great care with the appointment of a chairman. I was told that I could turn candidates down but would need substantial reasons to do so. Meanwhile Trevor Swete of Hill Samuel was passing through warnings, *sotto voce*, that BL thought that I was being too demanding in setting the terms of our privatisation, and that I was being pursued by Ray Horrocks, tomahawk in hand, in case I made a slip.

So I felt quite relieved when I met the BL-anointed candidate, Hamish Orr-Ewing. He had a distinguished family background, and was one of the very many Ford executives claiming leadership of the successful Ford Cortina project. He had spent time with BLMC, so he would at least have had contact with chaos and might understand what we had achieved. He was chairman of Rank Xerox, a jointly-owned private company, responsible for the sale of Xerox products in Europe, Africa and Asia. He was on the board of a public company as a non-executive director but he had never been chairman of a public company.

This last point should have rung alarm bells, as should the bizarre management practices of the Rank part of his organisation. All I saw in him, however, was a courteous, knowledgeable gentleman who was the enthusiastic owner of an E-type Jaguar. By the Arnold Weinstock test, he seemed an unlikely assassin. He was duly appointed.

We gave John Edwards *carte blanche* in choosing a non-executive finance man able to chair our audit committee, and, most importantly, able to guide him in the arcane practice of formulating our accounts as a public company. He needed a professional finance director and he chose Ted Bond, the finance director of the Beecham Group. It was an inspired choice.

The all-important Jaguar board consisted of the above two non-executives and Ray Horrocks from BL, and I was to be joined by John Edwards and Graham Whitehead as the Jaguar executives. To some extent the non-executives had control of the board, in that the chairman, Orr-Ewing, had a casting vote.

The prospectus told the exciting story of Jaguar's revival, and reflected well the direction we were aiming to take. Quality had continued to improve and as confirmation of that, we were now offering a two-year warranty in the United States. Warranty costs were now an easily-controllable item. Productivity was now 3.4 cars per employee and continuing to rise, with more to come when the XJ40 was in production – and the launch of this seemed under control.

The workforce was well-motivated and would have a generous share scheme on flotation. Sales were forecast to be at record levels by the end of 1984. We had launched Jaguar Deutschland, and sales in Germany were up by 60 per cent. Sales in the rest of Europe and the world would improve as well, once we took control of them. Product engineers had risen in number to 680 and this would continue to rise as we found capable people to hire; we were well on the way to the 1,000 we thought we needed.

Our racing programmes (discussed in more detail in a later chapter) were successful, and the Group 44 team in the US was developing an IMSA racer with our V12 engine, ready for an attack on the Le Mans 24-hour race that had been the scene of Jaguar's great 1950s competition successes. The dollar remained at an attractive level and exchange-rate hedging would protect short-term earnings.

The board. At the rear, from the left: David Boole, Jim Randle, Neil Johnson, David Fielden, John Edwards, Pat Audrain and Ken Edwards. Seated: Mike Beasley, myself and Graham Whitehead. (Philip Porter Archive)

After a gap of many years, we returned to Jaguar's happy 1950s hunting ground, Le Mans, with Group 44 running the XJR-5 there in 1984 and 1985. (Philip Porter Archive)

Jaguar management was allowed to appoint an adviser for the privatisation, and we chose George Magan of Morgan Grenfell. He began to introduce a more canny approach to our dealings with BL. 'Why are you helping them sell the IPO? All you are doing is helping BL to drive up the price,' he told us. 'Start warning the potential shareholders of the risks. Stop helping. Let BL do the selling. Remember when you have got a share price you have to learn how to defend it.' This was the opening advice of what turned out to be a long-term partnership.

Back at BL, the tomahawk was still out. Ray Horrocks had extremely onerous three-year contracts drawn up. They contained non-compete clauses potentially rendering us penniless if we left the company. Ray had decided that instead of giving the executives generous incentive schemes, it would be cheaper to chain us to the company with these three-year contracts.

The secretarial grapevine warned us that Ray was thundering up the motorway demanding my signature or my resignation. I had our Jaguar-US lawyer look at the contracts and he was vastly amused.

'Sign 'em,' he said over the telephone. 'English law abolished slavery 150 years ago. You will have no difficulty breaking these contracts; I don't think they would be enforceable in any jurisdiction. But try to laugh him out of them. Say you can't ask any of your colleagues to sign them. And when you've done that, ask him if he is forcing you to sign yours. That'll put him on the spot.'

When Ray arrived, we settled down to discuss the contracts before the board meeting to sign off the prospectus. He had worked up a fair head of steam, so I thought it wise for me to make a start, which I did in a sort of conspiratorial way.

'Ray, I don't know who is passing these contracts to us, but when I analyse them with my books on contract law, I can only see an onerous one-way obligation. Where are the performance schedules from the company? Where are the payments if we remove the directors' means of livelihood? What it says in my books is that without obligations both ways, there is not an enforceable contract. Look, I can't force my subordinates to sign these contracts, and if I do, how can I forbid them to take legal advice?' I shook my head. Ray was not pleased, and told me I was holding up the issuing of the prospectus.

'Look, these guys don't want to run away,' I said to him. 'They could have done that when things were bad in 1980.' Ray then asked me what I suggested as an alternative. I said, 'Well, why not say that they have signed mutually-agreeable three-year contracts? I think that those are the only ones that people normally sign – that is, if they don't have a gun held to their heads.'

We never got around to just me having to sign the contract. When I had taken myself out of the equation, everything had calmed down and we moved on to complete the prospectus. There was only one thing missing, the share price, and that was BL business and out of our control.

BL would still not tell me the share price on offer, nor what share schemes the senior executives would have, but it insisted on putting me up in front of the investors. George Magan and I prepared a carefully-worded and neutral speech, and to my astonishment nobody believed any of the reservations on Jaguar's future prospects that I outlined.

The speech to the City started by saying that Jaguar represented a rich spectrum of risk and opportunity, and carefully described all the risks. This prudent downplaying of our prospects was, however, undermined by the analysts. When I saw their reviews of the risks, they had subtly changed them into confirmations of our competence. On the vexing issue of the XJ40, they concluded that as I had left no stone unturned in trying to make it a success, it would inevitably be a success.

My final involvement in the conditions set for the IPO was a painful discussion with Ray on the executive share scheme. Compared to subsequent IPOs, our scheme was extremely modest. He shook his head in disbelief when I pointed out that it was normal for there to be some shares given to the senior executives as reward for success to date.

'What! You mean that British taxpayers would give shares to you,' he thundered. 'The whole idea is preposterous.' Whatever shares we got we had to pay for, or else were options on future performance.

BL also stripped us of all our cash. We were forced to pay back the £100 million that the Government had lent us. Looking at my own balance sheet, running from the moment I arrived at Jaguar, BL had got all its money back. To BL, Jaguar had given a positive cashflow and whatever BL got from the IPO was all cash in hand. But BL was a poor place in which to invest that money, I thought. It would have been better had it stayed with Jaguar. As far as I was concerned, on a personal level I had nailed my colours firmly to the Jaguar mast, and any rewards I would receive would have to come from future performance.

The IPO was a complete success, with long queues appearing as punters put in last-minute applications. The offer was eight times over-subscribed. What a sprat! I hoped that the British Telecom mackerel was worth it. I was already ruing not having been able to make it a private purchase. There was a final hiccup before the day's end: the Government had not paid for its Golden Share.

It was symbolic that I had to pay the launch price of £1.65, for the share, out of my own pocket.

Hamish Orr-Ewing and I rang the bell on the day's trading on the London Stock Exchange. Our share price gently rose, so the IPO had been correctly priced. On the way home to the Midlands, I tried to create a scorecard of how far we had got with Jaguar.

Having tamed the shop stewards, Michael Edwardes and the Government had allowed us to manage our turnaround under their protective umbrella. But we were still losing cars through disputes, and knew there had to be a better approach than shop stewards, mass meetings and strikes.

Leadership was the key – and leadership by team leaders on the shopfloor is what counts. Statistical process control was the way of making that delegation possible. Were we doing that well enough to be safe?

We had to create the processes within Engineering and with Manufacturing that allowed the new product process to be successful and predictable. How well were we controlling the XJ40 programme?

We had had a lot of help from the Bold Brigadier, Charles Maple, and his QI system, and from BL's grading system – which I did not want to change – and from joint purchasing with other parts of the BL empire. How well would we manage all these things on our own?

We needed a new engineering centre, as we had outgrown Browns Lane. But at least we had got rid of BL. Or had we?

While our rejuvenated and much improved Series 3 saloon (sedan) continued to enjoy strong demand, the pressure was off us to rush out its replacement and we could take our time honing the XJ40. (LAT)

Chapter 11

Privatisation brings solutions...
and new battlefields

1984-85

Privatisation allowed Jaguar to do things that would have been impossible when it was part of BL. Not least, the notion of finding the money to fund a racing programme would simply never have been accepted. I regarded racing as an absolutely vital part of developing our engineering capabilities. Connection with a racing programme was central to the need to build up our engineering department if we were to strive to be a world-best business.

As an independent company, I knew that in our plans there could – and should – be a bigger place for racing. BMW always emphasised race-proven design, and the Mercedes-Benz racing programmes were legendary. Racing had been the key to Jaguar's development in the 1950s and had bolstered the firm's subsequent reputation. It had accelerated development of the XK engine and prompted the creation of our V12.

But our current racing programmes needed rationalising, as they were becoming increasingly expensive, and were hidden in our marketing budgets. This was something we could now begin to tackle. What we wanted to do was capitalise on the highly valuable and effective relationship between our engineering department and TWR, and take Jaguar forward to what had always been our long-term aim – a successful return to Le Mans, where the company had gained much of its prestige. The only snag was that this was going to be very expensive.

Back in the world of manufacturing, we had resolved our XJ40 timing issue, helped by the fact that XJ6 sales were still growing. We built a special assembly hall to construct prototype cars in substantial numbers, enabling us to develop processes and train teams to build the XJ40. We also established a rigorous testing régime, which we thought would finally nail our reliability concerns. We put back the launch of XJ40 so all this could be done, explaining the nature of our testing programme to our suppliers, and urged them to work with us and make sure together that we launched a reliable car.

Our UK suppliers all groaned at the delay, but they did not follow our lead in adding to their engineering capability in order to make better components. Engineering was never a strong point in most of the British motor industry.

One of our more enthusiastic owners at that time was Arthur Scargill, the National Union of Mineworkers leader. He had visited us, and we had serviced his car while he had wandered round the Browns Lane factory amusing everyone. He was a charismatic speaker. I explained to him that I had a dilemma. Our Castle Bromwich plant was run on both oil and coal, and needed rationalisation of its power supply. What was I to do in view of the possibility of a miners' strike? The two fuels were more or less the same cost but coal was dirty to handle and required a small army of stokers.

'Go for coal,' he thundered. 'Our coal!'

When I drew the potential strike to his attention, he said that if we worked together we would prevail, because nobody could withstand the power of the National Union of Mineworkers. The following day he reinforced his message with a long letter, much jabbed with biro marks. It read like a speech to a thousand men.

Highly alarmed, I gave instructions for the Castle Bromwich plant to be urgently converted to single fuel – oil. There was a limit to what I would do for a Jaguar driver. Putting our whole future into Arthur Scargill's hands in a power struggle with the Government was beyond that limit. That struggle had started just as we were privatising, and now his strike was about to begin.

Ian MacGregor, our potential financier from earlier days, now had his own request to me. He was Margaret Thatcher's appointed chairman of the National Coal Board, and he wanted me to join him on the board as a non-executive director.

I was anxious to help Ian because his fight would determine our future just as much as our own efforts would. I enthusiastically agreed, subject to my board giving permission. Unfortunately they did not.

MacGregor and the Prime Minister had to lead a fight that, if they lost, would destroy the future prospects of any manufacturing company in the UK.

Arthur Scargill's ideas could only work in a place of universal subsidies, and thus of poverty. He was trying to reproduce the USSR in Britain. There would have been no place for a world-class maker of luxury cars in Scargill's world.

However, we had our own strike to attend to, now without the umbrella of Michael Edwardes's leadership, and without being able to use the crushing logic of BL's losses to resist extravagant wage demands. We were on our own now. We decided that our nerves could not take an annual wage negotiation, so we proposed a two-year settlement. We had offered an increase bigger than inflation, with a proviso that if inflation were above the forecast, the second year would be adjusted. The offer was all we could afford commensurate with increasing the cost-effectiveness of the company, which was still lagging behind that of our German competitors.

Improvements had been made to pensions, and members of the workforce now had shares in their hands worth £700 each, which they had not had the previous year. Senior managers had briefed the whole workforce and we all had the impression that it felt that the offer was fair, and would be acceptable. But not to the shop stewards.

They put out a written flier. It was not incoherent – the shop stewards had clearly attended the briefings. They noted that Jaguar was profitable and hence we could not threaten bankruptcy to pull its members into line. We had a new-model programme to fund – something I noted with pride that even this bigoted group accepted. But the product engineers were staff, and had not contributed to the productivity increase, the shop stewards went on. The dollar strength was a windfall – I noted that item also with pride – but, rather inconsistently, they wanted most of that windfall for themselves.

Although our product price rise for 1985 was going to average 3.5 per cent, they wanted a 20 per cent wage increase.

This we had to reject, as it would put us on the slippery slope with which BL had been so familiar. The shop stewards immediately arranged their mass meetings.

We had been working with officials from the Department of Employment for some time, searching for ways of encouraging secret ballots as an alternative to mass meetings. The Department was not sure about this. Maybe tackling the closed shop should take precedence? So Mike Beasley took a senior department official to observe our mass meeting. They were peering through the bushes and they saw the following scene.

There were about 2,000 people, mostly men, milling around. The chief shop steward shouted at them through a hand-held loudhailer, with a row of heavies staring intently at the crowd in front of him. Clearly, few people could hear what was going on.

The chief shop steward ended his tirade: 'We have been made a derisory offer by this miserly company. Those scabs who want to accept it, stand over there' – and he pointed to a place somewhere in the distance. 'And those who want to reject it, stand firm with their brothers, right here!' In spite of the fact that the heavies were hissing 'Scabs, scabs', 20 or 30 brave men did go and 'stand over there'.

'We'll win this,' Mike whispered to the Department of Employment official, who was aghast. So we did, but not until we had lost production of 1,000 cars, and the disgruntled workforce finally insisted on coming back to work, against the advice of their shop stewards. The Department, led by Secretary of State Norman Fowler, eventually introduced secret ballots, with sequestration of union assets to pay damages in the event of unions striking without ballots.

With exquisite subtlety in the order in which it was done, they then introduced legislation to control picketing to six people, thus preventing violence against people wishing to go to work. This allowed the secret ballot to be the final choice without the intimidation inherent in picketing. Finally, closed shops were abolished. The closed shop had allowed the shop stewards to impose their will on their poor members, as absolute tyrants – for without a union card you had no job.

The legislation brought to an end the period when control of industry was by the shop stewards – and what a dispiriting time it had been for any company that needed to be internationally competitive. I would watch with complete despair as the workforce would just walk out, and the only notice I would get would be the local buses turning up to take the workforce home. The stewards knew they had to get that one right: they could not have the workforce milling around with nothing to do, or they might want to go back to work. The problem for me was that a strike could be about anything that the shop stewards chose and, as I would have no warning, there was nothing I could do to stop it.

The shop stewards had complete control of the mass meeting and thus of voting. Even if they lost a vote, that did not stop them. Once this happened at Jaguar. It was raining, and everybody had umbrellas, so with people under a sea of brollies nobody could tell the result. The shop stewards claimed that the meeting had voted to strike, and then of course the resulting picketing stopped everybody going to work. Only fierce demands by the workforce to have a new mass meeting allowed work to recommence.

The ultimate control, however, was the closed shop. If you lost your union membership, you lost your job. The shop stewards thus had great power, and sadly did nothing useful with it. Their simple strategy was maximum pay for minimum effort, a sad end-point for any complex human endeavour.

The Government removed this national disgrace. Its legislation restored democracy to the trade union movement and allowed industry to be competitive. After the secret ballot legislation had been enacted, strikes became a thing of the past at Jaguar.

Those people who criticise Margaret Thatcher for destroying British manufacturing might usefully reflect on whether they have got the right end of the stick.

Whilst all this was going on, I had a major issue that concerned me very much. The Jaguar plc board did not seem to function very well, and had offered very little help in our battles with the shop stewards. My non-executive chairman was also agitating to appoint more non-executives, which would give him control of the board even without his own casting vote. I wondered why he wanted these extra directors when the board itself

The level of testing of the XJ40 prototypes far exceeded anything Jaguar had done before and included extensive running in extreme cold climates. (Philip Porter Archive)

The XJ40 testing still included the traditional, car-breaking Belgian pavé, as it was known. All prototypes were camouflaged. (Philip Porter Archive)

seemed to have no clear purpose. His letter to me saying that he would desist for a while with this action, because I so vehemently objected to it, had misspelt my name, short as it is. I was now a non-executive director on another public board Foreign and Colonial plc, and I observed a very different atmosphere there from that of the Jaguar board. We all seemed to be colleagues at Foreign and Colonial.

Our projects at Jaguar were being approved by the board, for which I was grateful, but our many problems and achievements were never much discussed. It was almost as if our non-executive board members had a different agenda from that of the management. I gained the impression that they were not very interested in what we were doing. My chairman, Hamish Orr-Ewing, was also rather autocratic – he had wanted to run a press conference during a visit to New York, without telling me or even our US company what he was going to say. I had explained to him that at Jaguar, authority was expressed through the management committee, and that none of us gave instructions to anyone, particularly in public, without that authority. I had explained all of this in a letter and at a dinner we had together. If he wanted something done it should be done through me, via the authority of the management committee.

I gained the impression that he thought I was being impertinent.

I wondered what Arnold Weinstock would make of this non-executive chairman. Why did he want to increase his control of the board? I had no idea what his intentions were. I was even more disturbed, however, when Diane and I learned through Hamish Orr-Ewing's PA that he was supposedly spending a great deal of time on Jaguar business. Whatever was he doing? There was something very odd here, as my impression had been that he was taking no interest in Jaguar affairs at all.

I had been invited to lunch by our investment bank adviser George Magan of Morgan Grenfell. I thought George might be able to give me some sound advice about non-executive chairmen, especially since Hamish had appointed George as Jaguar's adviser unilaterally, without consulting the board. I acquiesced immediately, almost like Brer Rabbit and the briar patch. George had given very valuable advice to the Jaguar executives all the way through the privatisation process and I had great confidence in his judgement.

George was always impeccably dressed, and he was always calm, although he occasionally showed an impish sense of humour. He carried that benign expression held only by those with information that comes from a much higher authority, almost as if he should have been a Monsignor in the higher reaches of the Vatican.

This was a special occasion. George had invited me to the Connaught Grill for lunch, and he was paying. We discussed our impending AGM, the very first for Jaguar plc, and a few other mostly trivial things. I was relaxed and about to raise the subject of Hamish and my misgivings. As I started on my very expensive Dover sole, George opened up, with some uncomfortable pauses as he went along.

'Er… er… I have a little thing that has been vexing me… er… I believe that there have been meetings in the Rank Xerox head office with your non-executive directors to discuss Jaguar diversification. Have you any knowledge of this?' I could not tell whether he was tentatively asking or in fact accusing. 'None at all,' I replied.

'Aah… I understand they have been running a ruler over the Italian Riva yacht company, and the Hawker Siddeley HS125 corporate-jet division of British Aerospace. There have been others. This will just be the start,' he said, in more of a rush. 'I… er… think it is all entirely unsuitable for Jaguar. It's actually quite mad.' Again he looked at me quizzically.

I said I was completely baffled. What on earth did we know about any of these things? How could we make money out of them? The HS125 was losing money, I knew that, and what money would we use to buy these firms? What expertise did we have in these technologies? George told me he imagined that they thought that Jaguar had a lot of money. 'Look, I think the whole thing is mad. I think that Hamish has been a corporate serf all his life, and now he is in charge of a plc board he thinks he can do anything at all that he wants to do.'

I was fast losing my appetite. How could they make the board accept this nonsense? 'Maybe Hamish doesn't think that is an issue. He will probably want to appoint more non-executives, but it is not clear what he intends to do. However, it is likely that he now wishes to exert overall management control and direction of the business – that is not the job of an independent non-executive chairman. It would appear that the chairman is operating far outside his proper role.'

Meanwhile, what was I to do? I did not believe a friendly chat would save this situation.

'The chairman is clearly operating far outside his proper remit, and therefore the board must decide whether he should continue in the post. In my view the board has absolutely no choice, no choice at all. You must sack him.'

The calm, impish George Magan had gone. This advice came from the higher authority. I thanked George and left hurriedly, the Dover sole largely uneaten, and immediately rang our corporate lawyer, Michael Mockridge of Coward Chance. I trusted Michael implicitly. I gave him the gist of what I had heard, and asked him to take his evidence first-hand from George at Morgan Grenfell. I was still shaking my head in disbelief about it all. This was far too absurd. We agreed that we should meet first thing on Monday morning to make our plan of action.

That evening I gathered the management team and told them my tale of woe. John Edwards was the only one to take it lightly, saying he thought it was just a piece of silly nonsense. He thought Hamish and Ray Horrocks were simply playing foolish games and I should just talk them out of it.

He also thought that Ted Bond, whom he now knew well, could not be part of anything against the interests of the company, as we saw them.

Neil Johnson, who later became the modern British Army's first colonel appointed from the Territorial Army, pointed out that Ray Horrocks had served in MI6, and that his training would demand that he had an answer to the control aspect of this escapade, and sensed that he might be the guiding hand.

Ken Edwards, the personnel director and now also the company secretary, pointed out a very significant thing. Ray Horrocks was going to miss the next board meeting, as he would be in Australia. He had apologised for his absence, but Ken did not know whether Ray had given a proxy to the chairman to cover his vote or not. Ken was also the most ferocious; he had reread his text books on becoming company secretary, and he thought that George was right. We should sack Hamish, and it would be relatively straightforward to do this.

Finally John Edwards pointed out that we had our first AGM in 30 days' time and he was already printing our first annual report. 'Whose names do we put in the brochures?' was his very practical question. In view of John's query, it was ironic that we immediately passed a vote of no confidence in our chairman, which had been our lawyer's interim advice.

We were all very melancholic as we began to close things down. I apologised for having an insufficient rapport with Hamish to talk it out with him. Clearly, I had tried, but he had been unwilling to tell me of his plans when we had met over dinner to discuss Jaguar. I prided myself in being able to talk with most people, but I clearly had been unable to extract from Hamish his ideas about Jaguar's future. Clearly, in Hamish's world, the chief executive should be the last to know!

We had to see what our lawyers would say. As life would have it, that intervening Saturday my wife and I were to go to the RSC at Stratford to see Roger Rees play Hamlet. He was magnificent, and he channelled my passionate feeling of misfortune into the wonderful words of Shakespeare. I had rescued and recreated Bill Lyons's company with huge personal effort, and these people were going to steal it from me. I had made promises to the workforce that I was not going to be able to honour. I had huge problems – with shop stewards, with the XJ40, with wage awards, with new engineering centres, with everything. My new enemies, to whom we were paying directors' fees, simply wanted to 'steal' our company's money – money we had all fought for – and waste it on absolutely stupid things. We did not have any spare cash: we needed every bit for investment in the future.

I sat in the theatre almost exploding with rage and energy, but Shakespeare was speaking to me across the years. I sat spellbound in my seat as I heard the lines, 'When sorrows come, they come not as single spies, but in battalions,' and should I suffer, 'the slings and arrows of outrageous fortune' or 'by opposing, end them'? Hamlet was saying it better than me. I had to end them.

John Edwards and I met our lawyers the following Monday morning. I had John with me because his view differed from everybody else's. Together I hoped we would be wiser.

Michael Mockridge was far more decisive than expected. He had been thoroughly briefed by Morgan Grenfell, including by his own personal contacts there. From the very start he had been concerned that we still had the BL connection, with Ray Horrocks sitting on our board. BL was not honouring its Jaguar contracts with distinction, and as a result he did not value Ray's authority over us. He had been concerned with Hamish's lack of experience as the chairman of a public limited company, particularly as Jaguar was shortly to become a FTSE 100 member. He was also concerned at the managerial antics of the Rank Organisation, from which Hamish would have learnt poor habits. He was very clear when he spoke to us.

'You must sack Hamish. It is your fiduciary duty to sack him. He is an unsuitable person to carry out the role your company has given him.'

He went remorselessly on. 'I did not want to bring unnecessary complications into our early relationship with Jaguar, but I did not feel from the start that this was a capable board. I therefore left in place, in the Articles of Association, a simple way of sacking him. He has no official place in legal contracts, so you can sack him with a simple board majority. You will have to wait for the shareholders to dismiss him as a director, but it has been my experience that directors would rather resign voluntarily than face that sort of ignominy.'

I asked whether we should speak to Ted Bond, as he might be on our side.

'Don't risk it – you never know,' he replied.

I pointed out that Ray would be absent from the next board.

'Do it then,' Michael urged.

I asked whether we had a simple majority, and what would happen if Ray had given Hamish a proxy vote. 'Well, it's not as simple as that,' said Michael. 'A proxy only works for items on the agenda. You must therefore make your vote into a special resolution, which will not be on the agenda. Then you will have a majority.'

He peered over his glasses.

'However, it could be the case that Ray has given the chairman an alternate vote. Sadly for you, that covers everything, and then you will not have a simple majority.' I asked what we would do then.

'Pray that each of you has a stronger bladder than he has,' was Michael's reply. 'When the first person leaves the room, the majority will change. Then you strike, appoint more directors and control the board.'

All this seemed very underhand, but Michael reassured us. 'No, it's my

---

Hamish Orr-Ewing had been programme manager of the tremendously successful Ford Cortina in the early '60s and then became chairman of Rank Xerox in 1980, joining Jaguar as non-executive chairman in 1984. (LAT)

When I went to the theatre in Stratford, I found Hamlet, played wonderfully by Roger Rees, enunciating my innermost thoughts powerfully and movingly. It was a catalyst to action. (Donald Cooper/Rex Features)

belief that Hamish intended to find a way of sacking you, John, then he'd control the board, and could create his conglomerate, of which he – or more likely Ray – would be the boss. That is what Morgan Grenfell has assured me would have been your collective fate.'

Michael looked at me.

'In my opinion, it's him or you.' He explained his strategy. He personally would remain our company's legal adviser, and would have the fiduciary responsibility to give precise legal advice to the board, including to Hamish. His assistant Peter Charlton, who eventually became senior UK partner of Coward Chance, would help us write the script for our fateful board meeting.

I fussed about hither and thither over the next week before the meeting. Hamish was older than we were and what if he had a heart attack or stroke during our verbal assault on him? We decided to have the company doctor on hand, with oxygen cylinders and suchlike. He displayed an almost indecent eagerness when we told him what it was all about.

David Boole was primed. He was ready to brief the world's press in a carefully-worded statement that would say that happily Hamish's work was done and he was ready to pass on the baton.

We had the two directors to be promoted onto the board – and thus give us board control – ready to step into the breach. Ken Edwards, as company secretary, would already be in the room, and Mike Beasley would be next door, waiting with the oxygen.

The board meeting started. After the preliminaries of noting that Ray Horrocks was absent, I interrupted Hamish's flow, reading from my script. 'Mr Chairman, I have very bad news for you. On Friday the management committee passed a resolution of "absolute no confidence" in your leadership, which carries with it a request for your resignation as chairman.'

Hamish was taken aback, predictably enough. 'This is a schoolboy prank,' he said. 'Please grow up. I have absolutely no intention of doing that. Let's now get on with the meeting.'

I read on. 'In that case, I have been instructed to put the resolution to this board that you are to be dismissed as chairman,' I said.

'Not so fast,' he responded. 'I have a proxy vote in my hand from Mr Horrocks, giving his authority to me.'

I noted with relief that he had said it was a proxy vote and not an alternate directorship. 'We have Michael Mockridge on hand to give you any advice that you may need,' I said. 'Should we ask him to judge the validity of this vote?' I had decided, as we were most likely to win, to be as fair as possible and not encourage Hamish to leave the room.

Michael came in, quickly looked at the proxy, and asked, 'Was this dismissal resolution on the agenda?'

Hamish responded rather timidly that it was not on the agenda. 'Then I am afraid that this proxy is not valid,' said Michael. 'The full authority of an alternate directorship would be needed for that. Perhaps we should go outside and talk about it.' I was much relieved that Hamish left the room with Michael, and we could complete our task.

Hamish was dismissed by a show of hands, Ted Bond abstaining. I could throw away my script. We all turned to Ted. What had been going on in those meetings? He was rather embarrassed. He had wondered when we would be told about these discussions on diversification, and thought it rather odd that we had not been kept informed. The relief in the room was palpable, but Ken Edwards, the company secretary, called us to order and told us to get on with our business.

We duly appointed our two new directors and unanimously promoted me to be chairman as well as chief executive. I reassured Ted that he would not be the only non-executive for long. As soon as Hamish and Ray had resigned, he could help us choose two new non-executive directors.

All the while, I had been extremely nervous about our protection under the Government-held Golden Share. What would the Secretary of State for Trade and Industry think about this escapade of sacking our chairman? Also, as BL was Government-owned and we had some important contracts with them, including for the supply of our steel pressings, we expected the Government to make sure that these contracts were honoured. I had discussed my nervousness with the chief executive of Morgan Grenfell, Christopher Reeves, and he had asked Sir Peter Carey, the former Permanent Secretary of the Department, to brief the Secretary of State about the departure of our chairman, and to say that we, the company, were blameless in the enterprise. Indeed Morgan Grenfell knew more about it than we, the directors of Jaguar, did.

With characteristic aplomb David Boole tidied up the business about our former chairman. He encouraged Hamish to talk only privately about his resignation, before Jaguar issued a fulsome press release, bestowing much of the success for our privatisation on Hamish's broad shoulders.

Now his job was done!

Michael then briefed the directors on the issue of the continued presence or otherwise of Ray and Hamish on our board.

'They are now in an impossible position, especially if you were to contest their re-election by the shareholders. Hold a special board meeting, give them the room to tell you what is on their minds, but make it clear that you do not value their continued presence on your board. Under no circumstance should you give any explanation about Hamish's dismissal. You owe them no explanation – they are the guilty ones, not you. The fact that you have no confidence in them – and after all, why should you? – is reason enough. They are both powerful people and thus dangerous, so give them as much room as possible to walk away with their own reasons for doing so.'

Michael helped us to construct as big a 'Golden Bridge' as we could. We held the painful and special board meeting where Ray and Hamish did say they would resign and intimated that it was because of our utterly bizarre behaviour. I noticed that neither of them looked at Ted Bond during this charade. There were no apologies, and no excuses, but at least no tantrums.

As the new chairman, I did receive a letter of resignation from Ray but it was so heavily redacted, I presumed by his lawyers, as to be almost unintelligible.

David Boole choreographed the dance steps for the upcoming AGM. The names of Hamish and Ray would still be in the annual report, but they would not be seeking re-election as they would have been obliged to do if they were going to stay on the board.

We prepared for the AGM with ferocious attention to detail. You cannot lose a chairman without some raised eyebrows at least – and losing not one but two non-executives at the same time must have looked very careless, to paraphrase Oscar Wilde. The board had not been redesigned – it had been butchered. The gossip columnists hinted at something close to the truth. What would the shareholders make of it all?

We made quite a show for our first AGM: cars on display, dealers taking orders, videos showing our racing successes. The room was full to overflowing. We played our latest employee video and started with our formal presentations, explained the resolutions and with quaking knees awaited our shareholders' questions.

The first questioner, a woman, asked fiercely why there were no women on the board. My surprised but true response was that women would be far too sensible to take us on, but I promised to look into it. Nobody mentioned our board changes. Half the questioners simply congratulated us on joining the living world, by leaving BL. Right at the end, a representative of the Jaguar Drivers' Club of Australia jumped to his feet and asked the shareholders to all stand and give the board an ovation for our efforts on their behalf. We swept him up to join us in our celebratory board lunch.

I thanked George Magan for his help and wise counsel. Only 30 days had passed since he had raised all those alarm bells with me. That chapter was now closed. In retrospect, I have thought how unlikely it would be that one of today's investment bankers would have behaved in a similar manner. He would probably have urged the mad investments forward, taken massive fees and hustled the failing company into inevitable bankruptcy, all with equal enthusiasm.

Chapter 12

A going concern, but with some peril

1985-86

I had found the actions of our non-executive colleagues profoundly disturbing, not only because they had been plotting what could have been the downfall of Jaguar in a secret cabal, but also because of the sheer lack of common sense in their plan. We would need all the cash we were generating to invest in Jaguar itself, not in loss-making unconnected luxury businesses.

Bill Lyons had been pretty tight-fisted when Jaguar was well run, often buying equipment secondhand, and then BL had invested virtually nothing in Jaguar for more than 10 years. We had to re-equip our factories. Just as importantly, the car business has always been cyclical, and it is vitally important to continue investing in new models all through the cycle, in bad times as well as good. Car companies therefore strive to have positive cash balances, large enough to tide them over the inevitable recessions.

We also needed a new engineering centre, and that would be expensive.

A more immediate consideration was that Ray Horrocks was in a position to do Jaguar harm. That is not to run him down: all is fair, I suppose, in love, war and business. In truth, I did not expect him to try and destabilise us, and we had already warned his major shareholder, the Secretary of State for Trade and Industry, that we were the injured party and deserved some consideration, if anything blew up. But to be safe, I decided to talk to my ex-colleagues in BL Cars to make sure of their continued support.

First of all, I contacted Harold Musgrove, chief executive of what was now Austin Rover, and of course our supplier of steel pressings. He invited me to Aston Villa Football Club and over lunch I had plenty of time to explain what had happened. He took great pains to tell me that we would continue to get our panels; he seemed so confident that I felt I could rely on him. In spite of the supportive attitude taken by Harold, we were not satisfied that in the long run we would be able to accept Austin Rover's poor-quality tooling and pressings. We thus put in train a project to create our own joint-venture press shop, which eventually materialised five years later, with GKN as our partner.

Moving on to other aspects of our relationship with BL, I knew my old friend John Neill at Unipart would stand by his contract, and Unipart was a competent supplier that we would be happy to retain. But I did warn John about the perils of privatisation. When he arranged the Unipart privatisation, it was as a private company, with him and his employees in control.

The BL European and Overseas sales company was moribund and doing a thoroughly bad job for us. I called in John Morgan. I asked him if he thought that in four weeks he could set up a sales organisation in every specified country in the world, except the ones we already controlled – in other words the US, the UK and Germany. He went away for a few hours and then came back and said that he could. John knew everyone in the motor business. You could not walk around a motor show anywhere in the world without meeting a friend of John's every few yards.

With meticulous attention to detail, he created, in only three weeks, a worldwide sales network.

He met everyone and he personally signed a distribution contract with every single company. He created jointly-owned businesses in the larger markets of Australia and Japan, and independents everywhere else, with Italy split into two, with companies in Rome and Milan. I knew Italy well and I concurred with this seeming oddity, as north and south Italy are like two different countries. We gave BLEO notice that we did not need their services beyond the remaining months of our contracts.

We had some engineering services from BL and we used their testing facilities and test track, but there were alternatives. I was now obsessed by making Jaguar safer – in the sense of healthy enough to survive – and safety lay in technical competence. There was a need to put our engineers into good facilities. They were housed in a whole host of wooden sheds, lean-to buildings, corridors and overcrowded offices, with their test rigs in nooks and crannies in all the plants. There was an air of great enthusiasm but it looked an amateurish sort of place to spend what would end up as a £50 million budget. We had to speed up our commitment to create a new engineering centre.

Our agents had found what appeared to be the ideal location. It was the Whitley site where, as I understood it, Armstrong Whitley had designed the ill-fated Blue Streak missile system. When the Government of the day cancelled the project, the factory had been sold to the Chrysler Group, which had made it their European Research and Development Centre. Chrysler had put in 24 engine test cells which had planning permission for 24/7 use. This was one of the many advantages of the site.

The new Chrysler chairman, Lee Iacocca, in his gutsy and quick-fire turnaround of the corporation, had sold his entire European empire to Peugeot, who had renamed Chrysler Europe as Talbot. The cars bearing the revived Talbot name would be derived from Peugeots and designed in France, so this now superfluous facility was put on the market. The site was cheap – but then every factory site in Coventry was cheap.

As I tramped round the factory, I was made increasingly gloomy by what was almost a taste of failure in the air and by its museum-like atmosphere. This was not helped by the demeanour of the site manager showing us around the site. He had worked there during its heyday and with vigorous arm movements kept re-enacting the activities once carried out in each building. My depressing thought was that maybe all us Brits were intended to be museum keepers.

In fact, I was so concerned by my irrational feeling for the site that when I met the Bishop of Coventry a few days later, I asked him to come with me and drive the ghosts out of the plant. He laughed at the idea of ghosts, but he did promise to bless the plant when we opened it, which he assured me was a sufficiently powerful action.

A dedicated modern, purpose-designed engineering centre was, I felt, crucial to our future if we were to design world-class cars. We created this facility at Whitley on the outskirts of Coventry. (Philip Porter Archive)

We finally launched the XJ40, known publicly as the XJ6, in 1986. Its success was vital to our continued existence. (Philip Porter Archive)

A very distinguished local architect, Scott Delamare, was responsible for an inspirational remodelling of the site, his last project before he died. I was always deeply grateful for the work he did for us. He instinctively understood my problem with the history of the site: fit for purpose was not enough. We needed a transformation. Turnarounds can often have ironic timings; when we eventually opened our fine new facility, we had already launched the XJ40 that ideally would have been developed there.

When Whitley was rebuilt and operational, we were visited by the Prime Minister. I pointed out to her that it was the only car plant in Europe opened that year which had not been subsidised. 'That is how they all should be,' she said in her usual forthright way.

After all the ructions described in the preceding chapter, we needed to complete our board. Our experience with non-executive chairmen had not been encouraging, so we decided to run without one. But we were delighted when highly experienced engineer and businessman Sir Austin Pearce, the chairman of British Aerospace, accepted our offer to join the board. He understood our problems and I felt was most unlikely to want to misuse our hard-earned money.

As the launch of the XJ40 approached, we were able to assess our progress as the inheritors of the Jaguar legacy. How far had we come?

Our barometer of quality was the JD Power survey in the US. In 1985 we achieved fifth place, behind only Mercedes-Benz and three Japanese companies and ahead of all other US and European car companies – a far cry from being last, as we had been in 1980. We gave five days of training to each employee and a quarter of our employees were now taking courses in our Open Learning Centre. Indeed, we were spending 1.5 per cent of net sales on training.

Productivity had continued to grow, and had reached 3.8 cars per employee, but even as we kept the improvements coming, we still were unable to keep everybody working up to the bell. The last 40 minutes of each shift continued to be unworked. But we had made and sold over 41,000 cars.

We now had over 1,000 product engineers, with annual expenditure of £35 million – or four per cent of turnover. A new styling studio had at last been opened at Whitley.

Our UK sales team under Roger Putnam, now that they had culled the dealers down to the believers, were generating some powerful marketing programmes. To get customers into the cars they had dealer-run events of great distinction: musical evenings at stately homes, clay pigeon shooting, lunch events to support our racing team.

We were one of the first car companies to run sales programmes for secondhand cars, thus protecting used car values. We even had our own Jaguar Silver Band to play at dealer evenings. Wherever Jaguar did its own sales and marketing, we were immensely more successful than the BLEO companies that we replaced.

In motor sport, the new XJR-6 Group C car had proved itself to be a winner, at the Silverstone 1,000km race in 1986, and we now had Le Mans in our sights.

Capital expenditure was £97 million, and profit before tax was £121 million – a record for a British-owned car company. We had £150 million of cash in the bank and committed borrowing facilities of £250 million. We were clear that our safety required cash. It was lack of cash that had killed British Leyland.

We valued our independence and had appointed Bruce Wasserstein of First Boston as our US adviser, prompted by the fact that over 50 per cent of our shares were held in the United States. With Bruce and George Magan, we had about the strongest advisory team any company in the world could have.

We felt that the recovery phase was over, and now we were a viable company. But in reality that was only at a reasonable dollar rate and with good market conditions.

It was exactly at this time that I received a telephone call from Sir James Hanson, ennobled as Lord Hanson, and creator of the Hanson Trust conglomerate. He explained to me, in a voice that must have said the same thing a hundred times, 'John, there is a great deal of sense in us talking – talking about the industrial logic of our two companies getting together in some way.' James was a very smooth operator and made it seem like nothing more than a little chat between two colleagues. I explained that we were very different from any of the other companies that they had bought, and that I could not see the logic, no matter how hard I tried.

'I am sure you are right,' he said. 'But why doesn't Gordie come along and talk it over?' Although it was called Hanson Trust, James and Sir Gordon White – later Lord White – considered themselves equal partners.

Years before, over lunch, James had explained to me how their system worked. Gordon bought the businesses very skilfully, from a cash point of view. The plan was simple. They always bought businesses that were worth less in total than the sum of the parts. James would then sell off enough to cover the original purchase price, before handing the businesses that were left to a small group of fierce cost-cutters who ran them to maximise cash and profit. Investing in things like advertising, new equipment, and research and development were ruthlessly minimised.

They had been extraordinarily successful and at the time Hanson Trust was worth about 20 times more than Jaguar. We were small fry.

James had been so disarming that I had not bothered calling in either of our two heavyweight corporate advisers, George Magan or Bruce Wasserstein. I thought that John Edwards and I could handle it together. And so it turned out, but with a bit of a scare along the way. John and I compared Hanson Trust and Jaguar. They might have been 20 times our size, but we spent more in capital expenditure than they did, and many times more in advertising, and on research and development. But to our alarm, John and I also noted that they could almost buy Jaguar with our own cash plus our committed borrowing facilities, but what was left would be very vulnerable to dollar and market fluctuations.

The very cash and borrowing facilities that we had put in place to make us safe also made us attractive to corporate raiders like James and Gordon. Jaguar, stripped of its cash and deep in debt, would be a very weak company indeed. No matter who owned it.

The reason for the visit was simple. Gordon wanted Hanson Trust to go into higher technologies because they were running out of conglomerates and basic industrial companies to buy. We said we thought that was what they should stick to, quite honestly. Our end of the market was a frightening place. We considered that Jaguar was far too risky a company to have any borrowings at all – and this was how Hanson was likely to run Jaguar, with a high degree of debt, or 'gearing'.

Since 1980 the dollar had gone from $2.40 to $1.20 to the pound, thus doubling or halving revenue, depending from which end of the telescope you looked at things. The US and UK luxury car markets fluctuate by 20-30 per cent in any economic cycle. We had just spent £200 million on a new model, almost half our net worth. What if it were a flop? Jaguar had spent very little in recent years, and we now needed to spend at least £500 million to bring all our facilities up to date.

These were all powerfully dissuasive arguments. But the killer, from Gordon's point of view, was that he would not have a clean fight. General Motors, BMW and probably Ford all wanted to buy Jaguar. The price would very quickly be pushed up beyond their business model.

Over lunch Gordon tried one last throw. How about Jaguar making a cosy deal, with Hanson providing a safe port in a storm if we got into trouble? I then explained what a wild, angry horse a car company was when it got into trouble. Jaguar had been losing £50 million per year when I joined it. Nobody but governments could absorb losses like that.

At the close Gordon said he agreed with us and that he and James would take no further interest in Jaguar. He shook our hands and that was it.

John and I, however, did smell trouble. Not only were we attractive to bigger car companies, we would also be vulnerable to unscrupulous corporate raiders. As soon as we had launched the XJ40, we needed to find a bigger and wealthier company with whom we could co-operate.

As a postscript to the Hanson Trust talks, we invited Gordon and James to the City launch for the XJ40 in London. They sat in the front row. At a break in our presentation, they both stood up, congratulated Jaguar on the new car, and each one then placed orders for 100 cars, James for his UK executives and Gordon for his US executives.

Chapter 13

The XJ40

1986

The XJ6, the car that would assure Jaguar's survival and return to health, was launched in 1968 by a design team at the height of its game.

What a team! Bill Lyons was the designer, in the sense of creating the look of the car. His design process was unique. He designed in steel from sketches with bits of hand-formed sheet metal propped up here and there, and then created a full-scale metal model. Everything improved as he went on; the reality was always much better than the model. His Mk 2 was better than the Mk 1, the S2 XJ6 better than the S1, the XK 140 better than the XK 120 and the E-type was a beautiful development of Malcolm Sayer's C-type and D-type. He relished detail.

When he was helping us with the detailing of the XJ40, he would throw his stick to one side when he entered the styling studio, shed 20 years from his age and delightedly boss us all about. I remember once saying that I was not sure about the headlamp treatment losing the by-then traditional Jaguar arrangement of four round lamps.

'But I am,' he very firmly replied.

If Lyons was cautious when it came to spending money, he was ultra-cautious on tooling for new models, and this was one of the reasons why there was so much lead filling on the XJ6 body. Much of the E-type was made with temporary plastic tools throughout its entire life.

If he was cautious with tooling, he was definitely stingy with manufacturing. We made our XJ-S cars on an assembly track bought secondhand in 1970 from Triumph.

Bill Heynes was his chief engineer and technical supremo from 1935 to 1969 and was responsible for the technical make-up of the cars. Through a process of steady evolution and prudent innovation, he engineered magnificent car after magnificent car.

Walter 'Wally' Hassan was the engine man. He was chief development engineer until he left to join Coventry Climax, where he designed Formula 1 engines for a series of British World Champions. Bill Lyons bought Coventry Climax in 1963, getting Wally back in time to design his V12 – an engine that would eventually win at Le Mans in 1988, 17 years after it had entered production.

The meticulous Bob Knight was responsible for final development. All Jaguar engineers lived in fear of Bob's last-minute adjustments. 'Last-minute' meant working through the night before handing cars to the press for road-testing the following day. The extraordinary refinement of later Jaguars was largely due to Bob – and in terms of refinement the original XJ6 was a recognised world-beater.

'Lofty' England, meanwhile, had run the racing programmes in the '50s and was service director. He and Norman Dewis, the chief test driver, told the team what was going wrong with the cars they were developing. It was 'Lofty' who took on the running of Jaguar, albeit for a very brief period, after Bill Lyons stepped down.

This team was responsible for creating a succession of magnificent racing cars, sports cars and saloons, hardly putting a foot wrong in 40 years of extraordinary effort.

Reliability was not a strong point, admittedly, but at that time Jaguar's British competitors were no better. The company was not too ambitious on volumes, and always endeavoured to under-supply the market. It was content to sell from 25,000 to 30,000 cars per annum, and was always profitable. Lyons took further risk out of their car business by developing the company into a vehicle conglomerate, making Daimler buses, Guy trucks and Coventry Climax engines and fork lift trucks.

Whether they were preparing a D-type to win at Le Mans or an XJ6 for a press review, the austere perfectionist Lyons and his team prized excellence of performance on the day, be it a race or press launch, and that is invariably what they achieved.

In 1986, however, Jaguar was no longer a conglomerate, with other related products on which it could fall back when the going got tough: all the peripheral non-car activities had been swallowed up by British Leyland. We were on our own, and in making over 40,000 cars per year we were now well outside the old comfort zone, in a market that was much more fiercely fought than in the past. We were now spending £100 million on investment and £50 million on R&D – 'Research and Development'. We also prized quality and reliability – we prized our customers' satisfaction. These things were not necessarily in the remit of the old Jaguar company.

By the time we were given permission to develop the XJ40, all the old design team had gone. Only Norman Dewis, the chief test driver, was left. The XJ40 effectively started life in 1973 when the first full-size clay styling model was presented to Donald Stokes and John Barber, as an ultimate replacement for the then five-year-old XJ6. They turned the proposal down. It seems certain that they did not see investing in Jaguar as a priority: it was still profitable, and it was felt the money would be better spent in trying to turn around the mass-market Austin-Morris division.

Stokes and his men would doubtless have been amazed to learn that we were still selling the XJ6 – and profitably – some 13 years later. By normal car industry standards there would have been two or three new models during this time.

Throughout the turmoil of BLMC and dismemberment of Jaguar following the Ryder Report, Bob Knight and his small Jaguar design team held on to the XJ40 project as a symbol of hope for the future of Jaguar. It was all they had to believe in during this wretched time. Their Browns Lane home had been renamed 'Large Car Assembly Plant No.2' and BL management tried to absorb Jaguar Engineering into a central department; Bob Knight had even been offered the job of BL Cars engineering chief, which he politely refused. Bob tried to ignore everything else that was going on around him, grimly hanging onto his little team, and continuing to develop his XJ40 project.

Four legendary Jaguar engineers, from left: Bill Heynes, Wally Hassan, Harry Mundy and Claude Baily. Heynes, Hassan and Baily designed the XK engine during WW2 and Mundy joined them to create the V12, launched in 1971. (Jaguar North America)

Though he had been retired for some years, Sir William began visiting the Styling Studio when we were completing the XJ40 and gave us the benefit of his wisdom, long experience and great eye for style. (Philip Porter Archive)

BL tried to get Bob to put a Rover V8 engine into the car, so he designed in crash tubes to make the engine compartment too narrow to take the V8. Of course this meant that neither – at least at first – could we put in our now rejuvenated V12 engine, the most powerful engine in regular production in the world.

I picked up the XJ40 project back in the grim days of 1980, not only as a symbol of hope, but also as a goad to push the shop stewards into reform. Why should I try to get future investment for Jaguar if their intolerable behaviour and the impact they had on the workforce made it impossible for Jaguar to be successful? When we presented the project to the BL board we did not have the resources to design a new car adequately – we had probably only 20 per cent of the requirement – and nor did we have much idea of the quality of the work already done in the Bob Knight bunker. But the design intent was clear, and I seized on the project as part of my survival plan.

The XJ40 promised to be more fuel efficient because the body and engine would be lighter and the drag coefficient would be lower, although that meant losing the sculpted four-headlamp front and other bold Jaguar features. The specification also included a four-speed instead of three-speed automatic gearbox. Fuel efficiency was important, as US fuel consumption regulations were getting more ambitious, and we could not afford to design a gas-guzzler.

The new aluminium AJ6 engine was lighter and promised better performance, thanks to its four-valve head and a much more sophisticated engine management system. In one leap we were trying to catch up with our German competitors by having a modern electrical/electronic system, with the ability to add on a host of electronic wizardry as required.

Just as importantly, the car promised a considerable improvement in manufacturing productivity, as the body would have 20 per cent fewer body panels. We could design for easier assembly. We could make sure everything was designed to fit. There would be no more 'Birmingham engineering'.

It all seemed very sensible, but I was haunted by BL's inability to invest engineering and financial resources into its new-model programmes. We only had a tiny number of engineers. Did they know what they were doing? Could we create a world-class car with the resources we were putting into the project? The poor quality of tooling coming from our associated company Austin-Morris had left us with some design compromises that I did not like. But I knew I had absolutely no choice. I had to grab the project and get on with it, as a symbol of hope in the future.

The people running the project were Jaguar. I had to believe in them. At the time there were so many 18-inch shells coming at us from all angles that I had to let the XJ40 project look after itself until I could give it more time. Our decision to launch the new engine for the XJ40 in the XJ-S had proved wise, but it was also a sobering experience, as we had quickly discovered that it could not be manufactured adequately in volume. There was a huge gap separating design intent and reality.

I chaired the task force to deal with this and also instituted an XJ40 launch committee. All was not well. Jaguar had always been run on a shoestring, but those days had to end. A disappointing ride-and-drive exercise, when I thought that the XJ40 was not yet as good as the XJ6 Series 3, brought the management committee to the conclusion that at all costs we should delay the launch until we had built sufficient cars to production specification, and tested all production components through 100,000 miles and added more refinement. That decision meant, as recounted, that Jaguar was privatised in June 1984, before we felt ready to launch XJ40.

After we had privatised, I had a long meeting with Bill Lyons when we tried to puzzle out together whether to cancel the XJ40 and start again. Bill was much more positive than I was; in retrospect, I suppose that he was overwhelmingly concerned with the styling, rather than our more fundamental engineering problems. He had always left the rest of the development to his team. We agreed, all the same, that he should spend more time helping Jim Randle with the detailing of the car.

I had private words with our top sales people, Roger Putnam and Graham Whitehead. They also concluded we should go ahead with what we had. Finally, I put the question of starting again to our top 100 managers, and overwhelmingly we concluded that we should continue with the XJ40 but would build production-spec cars and test them until we felt sure we could safely proceed to volume production. We had time on our side.

The body-in-white facility at Castle Bromwich was entirely new, so we could build as many bodies as we liked without disrupting production of our existing models. AJ6 engines were being made as a matter of course for the XJ-S. As mentioned earlier, we had also built an assembly facility at Browns Lane to enable a large volume of production prototypes to be made, and to enable us to train the production teams.

The testing regime we instituted resulted in us setting up a cold-weather station in Timmins, Ontario, and carrying out hot-weather testing in Phoenix,

Arizona, and the United Arab Emirates. High-speed testing required 25,000 miles flat-out at the Nardo track in southern Italy. Mundane mileage work was done at the motor industry's test track, MIRA, including 1,500 miles on pavé, and at Gaydon, taking in 35,000 miles on the arduous 'third world' circuit there.

All components had to achieve 100,000 miles before sign-off for final production.

Major problems had to be reported to the XJ40 launch committee, which sought solutions in the same urgent fashion we had learned during our long fight for quality in the early days. The management committee had regular ride-and-drive sessions with these pre-production cars.

I remember being extremely nervous of our ability to discover the truth from the inevitable explosion of big and small problems. There was lots of enthusiasm, lots of optimism and a minimum of pessimism. Would this mean that we would end up hoodwinking ourselves that we had solved all the problems, both large and small? This is always the risk when you get too close to a project: you lose the detachment necessary. It is important to remember that it is not just a question of arriving at what works for you, as an engineer. It has to work for the typical customer.

In this connection, about this time I read of British Rail's experience with its tilting train. Development carried on right until the day of the launch party. The engineers were doubtless sure they had done the best possible job. The launch duly took place aboard a tilting train going from Glasgow to London. It was a fiasco. The launch party had to abandon the journey, with hideous motion-sickness, having got no further than Carlisle.

Where does the truth lie? Who possesses the truth in large complex programmes? Our existing model range was still selling well. When the management committee had reached the conclusion that the XJ40 was better than its predecessor and the XJ40 launch committee had reached agreement on all faults, and their resolution, I decided to put the decision to launch back to our top 100 managers.

Everybody was of a mind to go ahead, bar one. Norman Dewis was still chief test driver. At the meeting he stood up and cogently argued for more time. He still thought there were too many uncertainties. His colleagues were furious, but we elected to give ourselves six more months.

After that, we had to commit. The pressure to launch became overwhelming; the whole company was straining at the leash. The shop stewards were demanding more money for making the XJ40, but as the workforce seemed solidly behind the project we felt entirely sure of winning any secret ballot. So it was that in June 1986 we started production.

We had built up an extremely capable PR team under David Boole and his team used all their flair and imagination to produce a press launch of real style.

The road-test circuit had mountain sections over Glen Shee – snow-covered when I tried the route in June – and continued through the beautiful glens and forests of the Cairngorm National Park to Braemar Castle, and then back down the A9 to Dunkeld. It was a nicely balanced long-distance route that allowed the XJ40 – now carrying the familiar XJ6 name – to show off its excellent dynamic qualities.

At Dunkeld the Stakis organisation made available to us its beautiful Dunkeld House Hotel on the banks of the River Tay. It was an hour's drive to Edinburgh Airport, so we drove the journalists to and fro in a fleet of Daimler limousines. We pulled out every Scottish card in the book: haggis to eat... guests being piped into the dining room with 'thunderous fiery' readings from Robbie Burns... an impeccable Scottish menu for dinner... a malt whisky tasting... video shows of our testing programmes... even the piper walking round the hotel in the morning to wake up the sleepy-eyed scribes.

I attended every launch event and was able to tell the Jaguar story so far, about how much care we had taken with the car and how much it meant to every single person at Jaguar.

It was a formidably successful launch. The journalists not only loved the car, but also the exquisite courtesy with which they had been treated.

The management committee was ecstatic because in three weeks of extremely hard driving – by mostly expert drivers, admittedly – we had suffered virtually no failures. Peter Taylor, the maestro running the press fleet, was very confident in the durability of the new car. He also pointed out a lucky omen: the Italian journalists had not crashed a single car!

We launched first to the UK and the 'Rest of the World' as we called it. North America would follow six months later. Already our sales teams and their dealers were considerable showmen. The launch events were hugely successful and we had overwhelming demand for our new XJ6.

Unfortunately, I allowed Manufacturing to hire more people, to crank up output to meet this early clamour for the car. My action was understandable:

when the original XJ6 had been launched in 1968 – and the XJ12 in 1972 – the waiting lists became so long that customers started to lose patience, and in some instances turned to more readily-available competitors. All the same, I should have followed my instinct on protecting quality and not got carried away with ratcheting up production too soon.

I attended many of these launch events and always anxiously quizzed the service managers about their experiences. 'As Jaguar launches go, everything is going well,' they tended to say. I was slowly calming down, but I failed to catch the reservation, 'as Jaguar launches go'.

Meanwhile, the North American press launch was in Tucson, Arizona. Again, it was a huge success, with brilliant scenery and great showmanship – simply everything went to plan.

I remember well one incident. This immense journalist, about 6ft 3in tall and weighing around 350 pounds, was walking purposefully towards my beautiful car, which looked far too sleek and low to the ground to take him. I wondered whether I should try to talk him out of the attempt. However, I had reckoned without his self-consciousness about his size: he squeezed himself in with almost elegant grace. When I asked him how he felt, he replied, 'Fine. Just fine.' Everyone a winner, I thought.

We had wonderful launch events all over the globe. I was particularly keen to do well in Japan. We were beginning to source many components with Japanese suppliers and I liked to balance currencies where we could. The British embassy was an ideal location for displaying our cars in central Tokyo. Alas, the ambassador thought this an absurd and undignified use of HMG's property.

Luckily, I attended an event in London, a function thrown by Sir Geoffrey Howe, the Foreign Secretary, at which he made it crystal clear to the gathered assembly of ambassadors and businessmen that one of the prime jobs of

---

The XJ40 launch and celebrations took many forms and included the workforce whose support was, of course, vital to the car's success. (Philip Porter Archive)

The press sampled the XJ40 on Scotland's wonderful roads and enjoyed great hospitality at our chosen hotel in Dunkeld. (Philip Porter)

16th SEPTEMBER 1983
THE 1st (FOUR) XJ40s
Who said it couldn't be done?

ambassadors – if not *the* prime job – was to support trade. I thought this an ideal time to raise again the issue of where we would launch our car in Japan. Both Geoffrey and the ambassador agreed that the Tokyo embassy was the ideal location. I thought that this was a thoroughly modern government: even ambassadors could change their minds.

At the launch at the embassy a representative of MITI, Japan's all-powerful Ministry of International Trade and Industry, asked me whether there was anything else that could be done to help us import our cars into Japan. 'Well, you could ask the Government to stop examining our cars individually and give us type approval for them all – as every other country does,' I said in a low voice. He grimaced, but agreed it could be done for a manufacturer as small as Jaguar.

Trouble did not hit until after the launch events for some of the huge US dealers. Many of them were selling 100 cars a month, way beyond the volumes of previous troubled times. They were used to handling problems with five or six cars a month, but not 100 – and customers were alas experiencing an unusual number of problems with the cars. It struck home when I visited my old friend Gene Fisher in Dallas Fort Worth. We had encouraged him to spend millions of dollars on new premises, and we were letting him down. He had his Texas finery on, but he was not a happy man at his party following the launch.

I had a deeply troubled night's sleep before I flew back to the UK. Our design intent was not robust enough and was still being let down by poor manufacturing processes.

I was to blame, even if I had created a company that was good at fixing problems. Give me a list of problems, and I will motivate everyone to put things right. But we should not have had the problems in the first place. Back at Browns Lane we began an analysis.

Fundamentally, there were three kinds of problem. Firstly, the testing had been naïve. In testing, the cars were in motion continuously, driven by professional drivers, and covered in camouflage. All of those things contributed to oversights, the camouflage covering some potential water leaks, for example. In the 20 days of transit to the USA, the complicated electrical system slowly drained the battery. To make matters worse, the heavy-duty battery specified after cold-weather testing in Canada had densely packed elements which silted up during the voyage, so reducing the battery capacity. The batteries never really recovered after this, and were a constant problem.

Of course, during the testing programme, the cars were in constant use and never suffered from this silting problem. Clearly we had to change the battery. The test drivers tended to ignore refinement issues, feeling that their job was above all to achieve 100,000 trouble-free miles, and not to be overly critical of notions such as refinement.

Consequently the Dunlop Denovo 'run flat' tyres did not ride as well as the previous XJ6's Pirelli tyres. They were 'run flat' to avoid our customers having to resort to the spare wheel in difficult or dangerous places, but they did not drive like Jaguar tyres – and they still suffered from malformation in transit. They would have to be changed.

The second problem area was created by our UK suppliers, few of which were capable of designing new products 'right first time'. Further to this, though, we had not adequately shared our testing programmes with them. We therefore had a litany of niggling complaints familiar from our experience with the Series 3 XJ6.

The third set of problems concerned poor process controls within Manufacturing. It had been absolutely wrong to bring in a new model and ramp up production at the same time. Unbelievably, a random set of problems was also created by well-intentioned engineers who put supposedly stronger bolts into the car at the last minute, avoiding the testing programme. These corroded, failed and required recalls.

We suffered deeply from lack of discipline and lack of process, and consequently the failures had occurred in spite of all our good intentions. It was old Jaguar rather than the new: the press launch was great, the follow-through still poor.

At least we now had capability to put things right, having just moved our 1,100-strong Engineering Department into its new Whitley headquarters. The car was basically strong and durable, so we had the potential to end up with a good vehicle, which in fact we did. In total 208,000 XJ40s would be sold, making it one of the most successful Jaguars of all time. In the meantime, though, in the all-important JD Power customer satisfaction list we had dropped from the number five spot to number 14, or about the mid-point among the 37 marques sold in the US.

We had a lot of ground to recover. The management committee instituted some deep soul-searching and came to some clear conclusions.

Up to this point, all management processes had been home-grown. In this most complicated of endeavours, the development of a new car, our approach had been found wanting. We needed better processes within engineering but also in coordination with manufacturing and suppliers. An important conclusion was that we should encourage our suppliers to locate part of their testing systems at Whitley.

This pre-supposed that our UK suppliers were capable of adequately developing new products, and we were not convinced that this was necessarily the case. But our German suppliers were charging us more for components than they were charging our German competitors. It seemed, therefore, that in addition we needed a large-volume partner to help us extract better prices from the European components industry in order that we would become fully cost-effective.

We also concluded that we must upgrade our management systems. We had begun discussions with Myron Tribus, an associate of Edwards Deming, the founder of the Japanese quality revolution. Should we commit to introducing Total Quality Management (TQM) into Jaguar? The questions piled up.

We also were mindful of global warming and the potential requirement, at some stage, for a 50mpg high-performance engine. Environmental demands – and those for ever-better safety in a crash – were adding to the engineering load. Would we have the resources to develop our own solutions? Or should it be done together with a partner? Should we look for a big brother to help us plan our future?

We regarded Toyota as the most capable car company in the world, and we aspired to be the best luxury car company in the world. Should we seek talks with them? We knew they were considering starting car assembly in the UK and we knew that they were developing their own luxury model: they had used some of the same testing stations as us.

Could there be a synergy here, between Jaguar and Lexus, their forthcoming luxury brand?

A great deal rested on the success of the XJ40 saloon, here seen by the Pacific Ocean. (Philip Porter)

The quiet roads of Scotland, framed by stunning scenery, were perfect for the media to assess the merits of the all-new XJ40. (Philip Porter)

Chapter 14

Working with government, looking for friends – and 'TQM'

1987-88

The urgency of our XJ40 'recovery programme' took all our energy, but it was familiar ground and the improvements came through quickly. Our UK dealers wondered what we were making all the fuss about, for they had record sales of 14,500 cars in 1988, a 31 per cent increase over the previous year. New sales records were established for Jaguar in most overseas markets, with record sales of over 50,000 cars for the first time.

We found our poise again with an impeccably launched and very beautiful XJ-S convertible. Over 10,000 examples of the XJ-S were sold in 1988, almost as many vehicles as we had sold in total in 1980. At that time we were not making the XJ-S at all, and unsurprisingly many considered the car to be dead. Now it was one of the most successful Jaguar sports models of all time.

In the annual report I was able to say that we had manufactured more than four cars per employee and that quality levels were steadily improving again. I could also delightedly report that Jaguar had won both the Daytona and Le Mans 24-hour races, the most prestigious 24-hour events in the calendar. Dealers in the US were reporting that customers turned up at their dealerships with their new XJ-S convertibles as though they themselves had won the races.

With our quality improvements well under way, I felt able to respond when, with some other businessmen, I was asked to help the Thatcher Government's bid to be re-elected in the 1987 General Election. The group included Gordon White of Hanson Trust, Dick Giordano of British Oxygen and Ralph Halpern of the Burton Group. It was going to be a much tighter election than the two previous ones.

I felt that, as a manufacturer, I could not have asked for any more help than I had received from the Conservative Government. Its industrial-relations legislation had made it possible for UK companies to compete internationally. The laws had been introduced with infinite care, wide consultation and in a measured way that we knew had been supported by our workforce. The workforce was now in charge of its own affairs, and not being bullied by the shop stewards. We could even introduce new models without the bitter disputes that had always occurred in the past.

The idea of having a left-wing government coming back, with hints of restoring the closed shop and overturning the industrial-relations legislation, filled me with such horror that I was willing to help in any way I could.

When I saw the way the polling was going I immediately hammered my credentials to the mast with a submission on the front page of *The Sun* entitled 'Seven Reasons Why You Should Not Vote Labour'.

No businessman's reluctance to join in the political debate there! I wondered how many Jaguar employees supported my intervention, but I was emboldened by the fact that, without this Government and its legislation, we could never have been competitive and we probably would not exist at all.

A far less successful intervention was when I was asked to speak at the Cambridge University Union debate in defence of the Poll Tax. The idea of families paying their way in proportion to the resources they consumed seemed at first blush to be a reasonable one. But it was less convincing to a generation brought up on the idea of consuming resources according to need, rather than ability to pay. The idea was missed in the debate that if you had to pay for the education of 10 children, you might not have 10 children in the first place.

I retreated after a thorough whipping, having gathered very few votes. Right or wrong, this policy was not going to win votes, I reported back. I have often wondered why Margaret Thatcher continued with this ill-fated idea. Somebody was not listening to the electorate; doing the right thing, right away, is not always the wise choice in a democracy.

The Prime Minister was looking for ideas, not only to win the election but also to give her instincts for wealth creation more substance. We were all given homework and asked to report back at about two-weekly intervals. But if you had a really good idea there would be instant action. Margaret Thatcher was a very good manager, far more capable of getting things done than her immediate predecessors or successors.

The proposal would be discussed by a small group, which would include the PM and the originator of the idea, together with the cabinet minister and the senior civil servant most closely involved. The idea would be very openly discussed, and the pros and cons examined. If consensus was reached that it was indeed a good idea, then implementation was examined, and if it were thought feasible and desirable the politician and civil servant would go away and do it. They always reported back on whether the idea reached fruition or not. All in all, it was almost exactly the way business people behave.

When I was later president of the CBI, I had to work with the Blair Government. It was a completely different atmosphere from the Thatcher years. With Tony Blair, ideas floated around like balloons, being blown about by the wind. In comparison to the Thatcher Government, it seemed as if they had the power, but had not fathomed out what to do with it – rather like my shop stewards.

One idea that I mentioned to Margaret Thatcher was that British executives could not fully participate in the ownership of their companies in any meaningful way. They were too heavily taxed, even at 40 per cent, to build up significant ownership. My simple suggestion was that share options should be purchased at the option price, without tax, even if at the time of purchase the share price were significantly higher – but only if you kept the shares and did not sell them. Shares that were sold would be taxed at the normal 40 per cent rate. This allowed the executive to get the complete gain, without tax, from his efforts, assuming of course that his efforts had something to do with the gains.

Because I had discussed the idea quite widely already, I knew that the Treasury would hate the idea as 'tax leakage'. But Norman Lamont, who was then the Chief Secretary to the Treasury, took up the cudgel with his colleagues. He came back with blood all over him, but with the job done.

This idea really did reward loyal executives and did create ownership; sadly it was later rescinded by Kenneth Clarke, a Conservative Chancellor who was excellent in most other ways. I fear he was nobbled by his officials on this one. The obscene salaries paid to 'FTSE 100' chief executives today in the main bear no relationship to the value that they have created for their shareholders. The 'Footsie 100' is more or less where it was in the year 2000 and yet chief executives are being paid four times more than they were then. If the main reward system had remained with share options, such increases would not have been possible.

One of my pieces of homework was to recommend a new way of funding political parties. I presented a short submission on half a sheet of paper. Essentially it said that the weakest part of the current system was the funding of the Labour Party by the unions. Great evils, like the closed shop, had come about as a result. I pointed out that companies, now that they were expected to consult their shareholders on the decision, would not automatically make contributions to the Conservatives.

That left rich individuals making the big donations, and that was simply corruption by another name. I recommended that the simple research and election needs of MPs and parties should be met by the state. Otherwise all donations should be limited to £5,000. It was up to political parties to be popular enough to gain the funds they needed to be elected. In other words, they had to work at it – much in the way that Barack Obama was elected for his first term as President of the United States.

The Prime Minister was not amused. She actually stood up and walked around behind my chair. She kindly congratulated me on my brevity and said it should be an inspiration to any civil servants in the room that such a complex issue could be fully explained in such a short paper. But she said I was, 'Wrong! Wrong! Wrong!' and went on to explain that as the Conservative Party was much richer than the Labour Party, this would be a very foolish idea.

When I look back, I suppose I had indeed been wrong. I had answered the exam question as I saw it for UK Ltd. I still think it was exactly the right answer and believe that such a system should be implemented. But what I had not done was to come up with a cunning plan to improve the Conservative Party's chances of re-election. Even the best Prime Ministers are shameless at election time.

For a little while, I circulated in what were exalted places for a businessman. This included attendance at a Bilderburg Conference. On one occasion, I was sitting next to Paul Volcker, the Chairman of the US Federal Reserve, and he wanted to know what I did. I said that I made

Jaguar cars and mostly sold them in the United States. 'You make 'em in pounds and sell 'em in dollars?' was his surprised reaction. 'How do you know what you will get for them in pounds?' I replied that we sold the dollars forward at predetermined exchange rates.

Volcker pondered on this. 'So you're selling dollars you don't have, and I suppose someone is paying for them with pounds that they don't have either. Is that how it works?' I elaborated a bit more, saying how we tried to have at least $1 billion covered at all times.

He then asked whether the business was worth a billion dollars. 'No, and that's not the only snag, as we need to sell about $100 million every month,' I replied. 'The market is only 2 per cent real and 98 per cent speculation, so when we move we stir up about $5 billion of froth, and the exchange rate moves against us, so we have 20 telephones and do packages of only $5 million at a time, but all at the same time.'

For the next half an hour, he told anybody who would listen what strange tricks businessmen got up to these days. From my point of view I thought how important it was that policymakers had some chance to get reality checks at these conferences – although I was somewhat surprised that I was telling Paul Volcker about exchange-rate hedging and not the other way round.

The Prime Minister took a proprietorial interest in Jaguar's success. One area that I was growing proud of was Japan. We had gone into a joint venture with the Seibu Saison department-store group. The owner was a very singular and successful businessman, Seiji Tsutsumi. It was always a pleasure to visit Japan. Seiji was a delightful host, who took himself to a secluded and secret place each year to write poetry and novels.

Sales were up by 100 per cent. Business was booming. I had asked Seibu Saison to introduce me to Toyota to discuss areas of mutual co-operation.

In line with other motor manufacturers worldwide, Jaguar
invested extensively in robots for the manufacturing process.
(Philip Porter Archive)

The support of the dealers was absolutely key to Jaguar's success.
Here we are planting a tree to mark the site of a new dealership in
Ontario in 1988. (John Egan Archive)

I suppose we offered no threat but in any case we were very courteously received, and I was able to put my idea to Toyota's senior management. Essentially this was that Jaguar and Lexus took shares in each other's company and that we undertook joint development of certain components. We would get Toyota's assistance with purchasing and help them set up their manufacturing operation in the UK. The Japanese promised to give it all serious consideration and to visit Jaguar as soon as possible.

The visit duly took place, the visitors including Toyota's senior manufacturing and engineering directors. They were particularly impressed by the attitude of the workforce. They also approved of our efforts to modernise our factories, with the automated AJ6 engine assembly line and the robotised Castle Bromwich body-in-white facility, where we had invested £100 million, with much superior body construction as a result.

We all got on very well together, with helpful suggestions going in both directions. They were extremely interested in our relations with the workforce, especially since the Government's industrial-relations legislation had been in place.

Sadly, the discussions came to nothing. On my next visit to Japan, Dr Toyoda himself brought them to a conclusion, with the observation that such a relationship would be well outside the traditions of Toyota. Collaboration was much more difficult than ownership, he pointed out.

It was ironic: we were being pursued by at least three car companies, but at the same time being rejected by a company we ourselves were courting. Maybe this was not going to be easy, I thought.

In planning for the future we had already made a start on a 50mpg performance car. It would be a hybrid, powered by a small jet engine charging a battery, with all electric propulsion via four electric motors in the wheels, giving very exciting electric regeneration possibilities. The

The XJ-S Convertible was a no-compromise, fully open car which gave the car a pleasing style and was ideally suited to the warmer climes of California where it sold very well. (Jaguar North America)

This fine paining by Graham Turner shows the XJR-12 of Martin Brundle, John Nielsen and Price Cobb taking victory in the 1990 Le Mans 24-Hours, ahead of the sister car of Lammers, Wallace and Konrad. (Painting by Graham Turner, www.studio88.co.uk)

electric motors were covered by a patent owned by GEC. Maybe this relationship would work? This could be the start of a joint venture, with GEC managing the propulsion system, the manufacturing or perhaps just procuring all the electrical components. GEC was big and very rich. The future of the automobile business could well be electric and GEC could well be the ideal partner.

GEC and Jaguar executives started to examine the practicalities and everyone started to get quite excited – except Arnold Weinstock. Arnold rang me up and asked when one of these vehicles would be on the road. 'With the best will in the world, it's going to be 15 or 20 years,' I replied. 'Oh! Let's forget all about it. I'll have retired long before then.' So that was that. Our efforts to find friends were indeed not progressing well.

Whatever partnership might or might not emerge, we decided we needed to upgrade our management processes. Our chosen path was to work with Myron Tribus, whose company was associated with Edwards Deming, the father of Total Quality Management. We were going right to the source, the fountainhead of the movement behind the extraordinary improvement of quality in Japanese manufacturing.

The story goes that when General MacArthur became in effect the Viceroy of Japan after the Second World War, Congress would not vote him sufficient funds to revitalise Japanese industry. MacArthur knew from his previous experience of Japan that poor quality was the chronic problem of their manufacturing industry. Edwards Deming had been one of the towering figures behind the astonishing performance of US industry during the war.

MacArthur therefore brought Deming over to Japan to instruct industrialists in US quality methods. If the Japanese industrialists did not follow Deming's processes, their companies could not obtain import licences for the raw materials needed for production.

Deming went one better than insisting on US methods. He brought in TQM – continuous improvement through statistical control of all processes. The system proved to be astonishingly successful. In the 1950s Deming took a group of Japanese businessmen on a tour of US auto plants; they pointed out to him that these plants were not operating according to his principles. He replied that he had taught them how the US plants *ought* to operate, not how they actually did operate. He was the most ruthless patriarch when it came to his system, and Toyota managers had been his best pupils.

Before Deming would let Myron Tribus loose on Jaguar, he insisted on meeting our board of directors. Were we serious people? Was our approach going to be rigorous and complete? When that formidable hurdle had been cleared, we set about upgrading all the processes within Jaguar, in particular within Engineering and in the coordination of Engineering with Manufacturing and Purchasing. We sent large numbers of managers and supervisors on visits to Japan. We encouraged the leading shop stewards to visit Japan and try to understand where we were taking the company next. I will explain some of these ideas in the chapter after next.

As 1988 closed, we could feel a gathering storm in the US market, where demand for luxury cars was down by 30 per cent. Jaguar was not as badly affected as the rest of the industry, but even more worrying was the weakening of the dollar against the pound.

John Edwards and I started to work out how we should tackle what eventually could become a worldwide recession. How strong should we make our balance sheet? We still had cash in the bank, but we had been unable to sell our dollars forward favourably for some time. Should we draw upon our committed borrowing facilities to carry on funding our forward model programme? We had a facelift planned for the XJ6, and an F-type replacement for the XJ-S with a brand new V8 engine.

Should we continue spending over £50 million per annum on research and development and £100 million on new equipment?

At the same time as we were pondering these problems, John Edwards and I were on a visit to Washington, and we were invited to meet Don Petersen, chairman of the Ford Motor Company. He drew attention to our previous talks on collaboration, before we were privatised in 1984, and very politely asked whether those discussions might be revived, now that we at Jaguar were free agents. John and I, probably more brusquely than we intended, firmly made the point that we preferred to seek our salvation as an independent company.

We considered that, difficult as things were looking for us in the US, we had seen trouble before, and we were very good at getting out of trouble. We were also interested that Ford did not seem concerned by the downturn in their own home market.

Chapter 15

Racing

1981-89

At the end of 1981, when our turnaround story was just unfolding, a most remarkable man came into my office, demanding some time. His name was Tom Walkinshaw.

By now I had realised that there had to be a place for racing in the scheme of things. Our heritage here was very powerful. We were turning the company round on the back of a 12-year-old product, the XJ6. It seemed to me that the years of waste in between the car being designed and my team arranging to build it properly held a clear message: racing had given the old Jaguar designers the capability to create products that were better than those of their competitors.

I was also extremely impressed by the way that other manufacturers, especially BMW, exploited their racing programmes with value-added 'racing-inspired' extensions to their standard range.

But how could I reintroduce some motor-sport activity, when I did not even have enough engineers to design new products, and break-even was still only a plan?

We had a successful XJ-S racing programme in the US, funded by the Quaker State oil company and by BL's North American companies, and run by Bob Tullius's Group 44 racing team. It was enthusiastically supported by US management and by the dealers. Group 44 was highly competent and extremely cost-effective, and they built reliable if not necessarily world-beating cars. But I could not easily see how I could build this up to be more than a purchased service. Being based in the United States, it was simply too far away to be an effective partner with our Engineering Department back in Coventry.

Nevertheless, I supported North American management when they authorised Group 44 to prepare an IMSA car that could eventually go to Le Mans. This was a stop-gap but would, I felt, be a useful learning exercise. Mike Dale and Graham Whitehead also thought, astutely enough, that going racing would dispel ideas in anybody's minds, particularly those of their dealers, that BL North America was going bankrupt.

I had the chance to discuss my ideas with Jackie Stewart, the former F1 World Champion, whom I knew was still a keen observer of the motor-racing scene. He advised working with an ambitious racing team who had aspirations in common with mine, and recommended Tom Walkinshaw Racing as a potential partner. He said you got three things in one package with Tom: a very fine driver, an excellent engineer and a hard-charging entrepreneurial leader.

This clear endorsement was in my mind when Tom enthusiastically burst into my office. He was part tornado, part rugby front-row forward and part mystical leprechaun. He took his time explaining his case – as he always did – and told me that by some strange magic known only to him, we could, at admittedly great cost, make our V12 XJ-S win the European Touring Car Championship, with him as the chief driver.

This was his bold claim. The power-to-weight ratio of the XJ-S was better than that of the BMW 528 or even potentially the BMW 635. We would have more pit stops, because of our worse petrol consumption, but we could beat the current champion. The XJ-S was a potential winner, especially under the new Group A regulations for the European Touring Car Championship – he was very clear about that.

If Jaguar could give sufficient financial support, his TWR organisation could develop the car into a winner.

I explained that I had two problems. Firstly, there had been a Leyland Cars racing programme for the XJ12 Coupé, carried out by the Broadspeed organisation, and this had proved immensely embarrassing for our engineering department. The cars were never really competitive, and the resultant wounds still ran deep. Secondly, at this point we had no money, even if we were turning the corner.

That said, we were about to relaunch the XJ-S with a new, more efficient engine. Perhaps now was the right time to support the model with a racing programme – but only if the car were to be competitive, which the Broadspeed XJ12C clearly had not been.

I also described my long-term ambition to have motor-sport variants of our cars spun off as a joint endeavour with any racing partner. I felt at the time that not only was this in line with Tom's own thinking, but that we might do it very well together. I remembered well Jackie Stewart's briefing on Tom; he was indeed extremely plausible and inspirational, and I felt that he would eventually win round my reluctant engineers.

Tom was not even slightly put off by any of this, and he undertook to find out what had gone wrong with the XJ12C programme and, more importantly, whether the problems, if they still applied, could be overcome whilst remaining within the rules of the new ETCC Group A category. Tom, for his part, would in addition see what further sponsorship he could raise. We agreed to meet again to see if we could overcome these challenges.

The Walkinshaw people did their homework. They examined the XJ12C and the relevant engineering drawings, and they also interviewed some of its design team, so they were very well prepared for their grilling by Jim Randle and his engineers when they came back.

There had been two very major problems. The first and more difficult was the lubrication of the engine, which had been poor, with oil surge under cornering and overheating of the lubricant. Secondly, at 1,700kg, the XJ12C had been far too heavy for the brakes with which it had been fitted. With the XJ-S the latter problem was fairly easily solved, as with Jaguar help it was feasible to get the weight down to the 1,400kg envisaged in the rules and also to do some reasonably clever things to cool the brakes.

In general terms Tom pointed out that the Group A rules were new, and open to pretty wide interpretation, and he was confident in his team's ability to resolve the oil problems and win with an XJ-S. He had also raised

---

In late 1981 Tom Walkinshaw came to me and said we could win the European Touring Car Championship with the XJ-S. In 1984 he did just that. (Philip Porter Archive)

In the USA, Graham Whitehead (left) and Mike Dale were great motorsport fans and believed in the value of motor racing for promoting the Jaguar brand. (Philip Porter Archive)

further sponsorship from Motul, makers of synthetic oil – and a big help in researching and tackling the oil issue – and from a very capable and wealthy co-driver, Chuck Nicholson.

We seemed to have solutions to my concerns, so we did a deal. Maybe it was because I was fresh from negotiating with the dealers, but at this first meeting, for the only time with him, I got the better of the negotiation in terms of the agreement. He wanted a huge amount of money that we did not have, but I eventually offered payment by results – £30,000 for a win, £20,000 for being second and £10,000 for a podium finish – along with free cars and components. He took the deal.

Later I discovered, much to my cost, what a formidable negotiator he was. I therefore only discussed money with him just after he had got out of a race car, exhausted from doing a stint at the wheel; but he was canny even then.

I later discovered that things did not start well. The first two V12 engines given to TWR had been abandoned after a corrosion-testing programme and were in a waste-disposal site when TWR arrived to collect them. But Tom and his team were not deterred by anything – they just charged on. Their technical competence and sheer exuberance slowly won the Jaguar team over.

This was just as well, since immense effort was required from Engineering to enable successful homologation of the cars. Typical of how this co-operation worked was when Engineering remembered that it had homologated a wider rear track for a small series of armour-plated vehicles; this would allow bigger rear wheels and thus bigger brake discs. They co-operated on a fuel injection system that helped produce a record 390bhp for the Jaguar V12.

Tom's men were clearly bent on winning, and every single component in the car was weighed and judged for its suitability to be included in a racing car – and to assess whether or not its replacement was permitted by the rules. If not, the next question was whether the rules could be creatively interpreted to accommodate modifying or replacing the part in question.

After three or four months of frantic effort, the first XJ-S raced at Monza, and led the race briefly. Two weeks later, at Vallelunga, we took pole position and eventually finished third. I was so impressed by this performance that I authorised a special bonus, and TWR was paid as though we had finished second. We were on our way.

With immense dedication and skill, the TWR team continued developing the XJ-S, eventually winning at the Nürburgring and at Silverstone in the prestigious Tourist Trophy race.

Luckily for all of us, Tom did enough winning for the financial arrangements to work for both of us. We added up the column inches extolling these victories, and in terms of positive PR we gained far more than we had spent. Tom's racing programmes were a tremendous tonic for the UK dealers, and later those in Europe – dealers who learnt to be just as effective as our US dealers in using these races to promote sales.

Tom Walkinshaw's performance in leading his team in 1982 was a huge personal achievement. Not only had he beaten the well-resourced BMW team on a number of occasions, but he had done it on a shoestring budget, and at immense risk to his own business if he had failed. But for me he had done a further service: he had won over our engineers, who were once again involved in trying to design components to world-best standards.

BMW was also very impressed with Tom's performance. They announced that in 1983 they would race their BMW 635, an altogether more fierce competitor than the BMW 528 that we had been able on occasion to beat.

One little hangover from 1982 was that we were supposed to have built 5,000 examples of the XJ-S to comply with the homologation regulations for the championship, which was meant for mass-produced cars. In the 1981 model year we had not built any XJ-Ss and for 1982 only 3,900. But we argued that we were on a rate of climb and had components in hand and on order to take us up to 5,000 cars. The authorities were so pleased to have another manufacturer competing that our figures were accepted.

Given that we eventually ramped up production of XJ-S to over 10,000 per annum, I would like to feel that this relaxation of the rules was justified.

With profitability returning in 1983, our racing programmes became much more ambitious, with Engineering co-ordinating vehicle and engine development between themselves and Group 44 and TWR. North American sales were going increasingly well and BL North America decided to increase its investment in Group 44 and encourage it to further develop the IMSA sports racing car and take it to Le Mans. As to the power unit for the US IMSA series, the Jaguar Engineering department recommended a 6-litre version of the V12 engine, following work they had done on this with TWR.

We brought the XJR-5, which was in second place in the IMSA series, over to Silverstone, and hired Porsche driver Derek Bell to test it, thus allowing us to compare it with the formula-leading Porsche. We were off the pace to the tune of two seconds per lap, the main problem being that poor fuel efficiency, which is not measured in the IMSA series, would not allow it to be fully competitive in European racing.

I tried to visit as many of the races as I could. To save time, I hired a plane to go to the events in Europe. To help justify the expenditure, I took various VIP guests with me.

Monza, our first touring car race in 1983, was a real thriller. We had not yet optimised the aerodynamics of the racing XJ-S and we had immense, and at that time unknown, upward air currents under the bonnet. These forces were particularly violent at Monza because the car was reaching 165mph on the straights.

Towards the end of the race, Jaguar was leading easily, but being right in front of the pits we could see that the retaining pins holding the bonnet down had sheared. The bonnet was now flapping in an alarming fashion and Chuck Nicholson was having to peer over it, obviously losing forward vision almost entirely on some occasions. We hastily prepared a tape bandage and called him in. Out he went, now in fourth position. Unfortunately, the bandage sheared and the bonnet continued its violent flapping.

In one of the most spirited sessions of driving I have ever seen, Chuck, ignoring the fact that he could only occasionally see the complete track, proceeded to overtake the third- and second-placed cars and was within 3½ seconds of the leader when the race ended. The Italian crowd had gone wild with excitement, urging Chuck on as only Italians can. They surged round his car as he came to a halt.

One of my VIP guests said, when we were on our way home, that it was the most exciting day of his life.

In 1984 Tom Walkinshaw (top left) not only took the ETCC Manufacturers' Championship with his TWR team but he also won the Drivers' Championship himself. (Philip Porter Archive) I am clearly reflecting (top right) on our chances during this race. (Philip Porter)

I was fortunate to have Tom Walkinshaw and Graham Whitehead behind me, in more senses than one. (Jaguar North America)

Our marketing department also made careful note, and created a travel club for enthusiasts wanting to attend our races, in addition to the customers that our dealers took to the circuits. Motor racing was at that time very cost-effective for manufacturers to take customers to, as hospitality suites were inexpensive for the dealers, and we could take our own caterers with us. A double-decker bus followed us everywhere, dispensing meals and drinks to the Jaguar enthusiasts who would be there in hundreds – or even thousands at Le Mans. In contrast, in Formula 1 it is prohibitively expensive for manufacturers to entertain more than a handful of their customers.

We were competitive all the way through the 1983 season. One race I was particularly keen to win was at the Nürburgring. We now had our own sales company in Germany. Sales were going very well, particularly of the XJ-S and XJ12, and competition success against our German rivals could only provide a further boost.

We had won the previous year, but of course we were now up against a much more formidable competitor in the BMW 635. When practice was over, I took the opportunity to be driven round the magnificent mountain circuit by one of the drivers. As I was wandering back to our base, I was approached by one of the BMW drivers, Hans Stuck. He said that he knew both of our cars from following them in early testing, and had noticed that they had distinctly different ride characteristics.

He knew therefore that Tom was qualifying both our cars using only one of them for the qualifying laps; this was not allowed by the rules.

I tackled Tom, who immediately justified himself. Racing is all about winning, he said, and about what you can get away with on the way. Right now the second car was having its engine rebuilt, and could not be used for qualifying, so he had switched the race numbers from one car to the other. I pointed out that this was still his team, but if it had been a Jaguar team I would have been forced to withdraw at least the unofficially-qualified car from the race, if not both of them, to protect our good name.

He looked at me quizzically for a while and then he nodded, and said that we were both on a learning curve. I was gaining a lot of respect for Tom and from that point on we tried to discuss everything at issue, to make sure we had common cause, no matter what the difficulties were. I cannot remember any other time when we had a similar disagreement, and he did learn how to protect our good name.

The year 1983 ended up as more hopeful than successful, for in both our racing programmes, IMSA and Group A, we came second. Jim Randle and Engineering were now spending more time helping Group 44 improve the performance of its car, particularly to give it a chance at Le Mans. I could see that Tom Walkinshaw was displeased at playing second fiddle to Group 44, but I made it quite clear that winning the ETCC Group A title was a necessity, before he could move on to something bigger with a Group C Le Mans car.

Luckily, 1984 was a most successful year in every way for Jaguar Cars. We had floated the company on the London Stock Exchange and could start to fix some of the things that had been impossible to rectify as part of BL Cars. We could also now put our racing programmes on a sound financial footing.

To immense excitement, we brought Group 44 over to Le Mans with two examples of the XJR-5.

We were not fully competitive with the front-runners – and had indeed stressed that this was not a 'works' team and that we did not expect to win first time out. All the same, at the 12-hour mark we were lying sixth when a broken gearbox caused our second car to retire. Later research indicated that half of all withdrawals from Le Mans over all time were due to gearbox failures. Clearly tired drivers needed immense discipline to be kind to their gearboxes, which therefore had to be extremely strong.

Even though we had not finished, I did appreciate how heart-stirring it had been to see the company back at Le Mans, 27 years after our last victory in the famous French event. Winning this race was very important to rebuilding Jaguar's mystique.

In the meantime, Tom Walkinshaw's 1984 XJ-S team was doing increasingly well in the European Touring Car Group A Championship. They ended up winning eight races – including, very importantly, the Spa 24-hour race in Belgium – and carrying off the Championship, with Tom in addition becoming the Drivers' Champion.

One of the reasons we were so dominant was that TWR and Jaguar Engineering were working very well together. Their shared engine-development programme had created the V12 that powered the winning cars. They had also produced a four-valve head for the V12 engine, which now produced 650bhp and this had clear potential for use in a Group C Le Mans car.

I was impressed when reading the minutes of their joint meetings to see how willing they were to solve the various component problems together, as the racing programmes developed. They had cleverly and cost-effectively created special lightweight bodies for the XJ-S at the factory by deleting unnecessary parts not needed on a race car. Real development work was being done. Jaguar engineers were producing solutions for the braking and suspension problems experienced during racing. They were designing components that were being tested to the limit.

Clearly Engineering was now taking TWR seriously. It was starting to give the TWR team new components and cars for their development programmes and not tired-out used ones. This relationship was adding real value to our engineering capabilities.

I visited TWR on a regular basis and I was beginning to feel that Tom was building up a formidably effective organisation. Everything he had said he could do, he had done, and he had created, I suspected, immense potential for the future.

TWR and Jaguar had also formed a joint company, JaguarSport, to sell specially prepared cars derived from our racing programme, through our dealers, to the general public. The company was almost immediately profitable, selling in particular a jointly-developed 6-litre XJ-S, with styling we might well use in the future, we thought, on all our XJ-S models. The engine incurred little extra cost because it was made in the Jaguar factory with very few manufacturing changes from normal.

JaguarSport was doing very much the same sort of job that the Jaguar racing department had done for Sir William Lyons, in trying out new things ahead of their incorporation on production cars.

Where did we go now with all this racing activity? As an independent company, we could now put it all on a sound footing and not necessarily

---

Not surprisingly, we were immensely proud of our victory at Le Mans in 1988 and we shared it with our workforce by devoting the front cover of Topics *to this photo showing the winning car, plus the other two TWR Jaguars that Tom marshalled into position should the leading car need some 'assistance' on the last lap.*

TOPICS  JAGUAR

July 1988

Number 56

Photo: Motor/Jaguar Driver

have to hide it in our marketing budgets. I gathered together all the people connected with racing – Bob Tullius and Tom Walkinshaw, Jim Randle and our senior sales people, Mike Dale from the US, sales and marketing director Neil Johnson, but especially UK sales director Roger Putnam, who had held a similar post with Lotus and was used to funding an expensive racing team.

Our programmes were modest and came out of our marketing budgets. But we had two programmes. Was this sensible? TWR was next door, near Oxford. But Group 44 was in Virginia, 3,000 miles away in the United States. Not only that, but we had Formula 1 technology in the UK and we could certainly learn from the F1 teams.

I wanted a car to win Le Mans. Clearly TWR was best placed to develop the engine. Should they take over the Group 44 IMSA car and try to make it better? Or should TWR start again? I went into the meeting convinced that the Group 44 route would be the cheaper option. The idea with which we all emerged was that Tom would campaign the Group 44 XJR-5 that had raced at Le Mans. He would develop it as a Group C car to win Le Mans and, jointly with Jaguar Engineering, would develop the engine for his own use and also for use in the Group 44 IMSA programme in the United States.

Roger Putnam would search for sponsors for what might be only a modestly costly endeavour. Tom said he would give it a try, but reserved the right to go his own way if he thought that best. This large group all departed happily, assuming that we had squared circles and put quarts into pint pots and very cleverly produced a world-beating and appropriately low-cost solution.

I should have known Tom better: he did as he was asked for about as long as it took him to visit Frank Williams, the Formula 1 race-team owner. Frank pointed out that if Tom tried to win with the Group 44 car, it would be a development exercise on a relatively old-fashioned space-frame design. Porsche had been running their space-frame racers at Le Mans for 10 years at least, and extremely competent people that they were, they would always be 10 years ahead of us.

For Tom to win, it was argued, he needed Formula 1 technology, in particular a monocoque structure. His only chance was to start again and get ahead of Porsche. Tom was convinced enough to hire Tony Southgate, a very talented F1 designer, and assuming only that he would have to use our V12 engine, briefed him to design a Group C winner around this power unit.

This was done very rapidly and Tom came to see me with his entirely revolutionary concept. We had before us the design of an F1 car built around an immensely strong monocoque and with a semi-stressed 7-litre V12 engine developing 700bhp in a car weighing just 850kg. The only downside was that it was going to cost around £10 million to develop and also £10 million per year to race – and we should also be ready for a long haul, as it might take three years to win Le Mans.

But Tom was clear in his own mind: if we wanted to win, this was the only way.

We gave the funding problem to Roger Putnam, who had been responsible for raising the money for Lotus and their Formula 1 team. To find a sponsor, Roger hired Guy Edwards, the F1 driver who had helped rescue Niki Lauda from his burning F1 car during a race. He was clearly a man not easily deterred and thought it would be an easy sell, and off he went to do it.

Suitably buoyed-up, we committed to Tom's Group C programme. Soon Guy had found what he said was the ideal sponsor, who would prefer a long-term deal and would not be frightened by the cost. It was cigarette brand Silk Cut, owned by Gallaher. The UK-based tobacco company was a very sophisticated brand developer and would make an ideal partner. There was one major problem: what did we think about working with a tobacco company? I felt particularly sensitive to this issue, as I had just stopped smoking after a rather long battle to quit.

The management committee met to work our way through the issues. Roger pointed out that, if Silk Cut started the programme, it would stick to it as long as we were competitive – and Tom was always that. John Edwards said if we were going to do such a programme, now was the time to do it. With the current highly-favourable dollar exchange rate, we were making £10 million per month in profit. Tom Walkinshaw had never let us down, and his Group A performance had been outstanding against such a formidable competitor as BMW.

Tom was probably right. In order to beat Porsche, he would need every advantage we could give him, and Formula 1 technology was much more easily available to us in the UK than it was to Porsche in Germany. We were tending to go with Tom, but I was still acutely aware of the tobacco issue.

I decided to consult our top 100 managers. I asked for both cases to be put – for and against. The managers put the issue back to the management committee: was tobacco sponsorship the only way we could go racing? If it was, then go ahead and do it. The question was basically, who else was there but a tobacco company that would commit to £20-30 million over a three-year period?

Roger and Guy were quite adamant: we go with Silk Cut or we will not be winning races. Also the Silk Cut managers would be a positive force in helping develop the Jaguar brand itself.

Whilst all this was going on, Group 44 brought its cars back to Le Mans in 1985, and finished a creditable 13th, winning the IMSA sub-group within the race. There was great media interest. But what would it have been like if we had won? It reinforced our decision to proceed with our all-new TWR Group C car.

Tom set off at what was for him his normal extraordinary pace. He built his new car, a 6-litre XJR-6, and won his first race with it at the Silverstone 1,000km in May 1986. We were so impressed that we decided to gain economies of scale by entrusting the IMSA programme in the US to him also, gaining Castrol as a sponsor for a two-year contract.

This turned out to be a very important move. It meant that we could field more cars at Le Mans by entering cars for both teams. We would need heavy battalions to beat Porsche and we knew there would normally be three Porsche teams and often up to five more privateers.

The bigger we made the V12 engine, the sweeter it got. In 1987, with a 7-litre engine, the XJR-8 completely dominated the World Sports Car Championship, winning eight out of the ten races and with one of our drivers, Raul Boesel, winning the Drivers' Championship. I had stipulated, in fact, that Tom could not drive and run the team at the same time. Tom had fairly readily agreed: he said he only wanted F1 drivers, and the younger the better. But we failed to win Le Mans that year, all three cars dropping out and with Win Percy suffering a dreadful accident on the Mulsanne Straight thanks to a burst tyre.

I was at Daytona in 1988 when our XJR-9 Castrol Jaguar won a very exciting 24-hour race from Porsche. It was a flat-out contest, with the two leading cars, Jaguar and Porsche, never being more than two minutes apart. Our credentials were falling into place for Le Mans, and these now included beating Porsche in a 24-hour race. After our win, I was very amused that we had no champagne to celebrate the victory, but the speed cop we had hired to guard the compound had a brother-in-law who did. Very rapidly, crates of a US vintage turned up. This was much to the horror of Chloe Smillie, the wife of James Smillie, our West End London dealer, who forbade him to drink it, saying that it was certainly not fit for a distinguished Mayfair car dealer to imbibe.

Celebrations over, one of the drivers pointed out that Daytona was a much less demanding and frightening track than Le Mans, with less speed variation, less traffic, and as a result much less stress for the drivers.

With all this in mind, we took a formidable team with us to Le Mans in 1988 – five cars, 15 drivers and over 120 personnel, including dieticians and physiotherapists. One of the latter had developed a technique, which all the drivers found disconcerting but effective, of waking up the drivers for their next shift, and shadow-boxing the driver until he was so irritated that he would hit back, at which point the driver would be declared fit to drive.

The night before the race we had a dinner for the team, including the drivers – a huge pasta fest, on the instructions of the dietician. We were at the restaurant that Bill Lyons used. Amongst my guests was Pat Mennem, the distinguished veteran journalist, who had been Sir William's guest in the 1950s, as had John Baring, now one of our non-executive directors. Their travellers' tales in these most nostalgic of circumstances are firmly ingrained in my memory, including how Pat was given a lift from England in one of the race cars. Bill Lyons was always keen to demonstrate that these were normal road cars that could race, even if you were hardly likely to go down to the grocer's store in your race-winning D-type.

The more experienced drivers, such as Jan Lammers, had detailed set-up discussions with the engineers. Jan had gone for less downforce, which gave less grip on the corners but much greater speed on the Mulsanne Straight, where he thought he would be doing about 250mph. There is nothing more demoralising for a racing driver, he argued, than being easily overtaken on the straight.

He had also taken his duties as team leader very seriously; he had walked the entire course with his co-drivers to agree the way they would all drive their car, including the rpm to take each corner. He kept on stressing kindness to the car and care with the gearbox. One of his team-mates, Andy Wallace, had never driven a 24-hour race before and this was the first time he would drive at over 200mph.

Another driver, Johnny Dumfries, was an experienced campaigner and appreciated the merits of team discipline. He deferred fully to his more experienced team leader.

The day of the race started in remarkable fashion for me. I was 'President du Mans' with many duties, including a reception and lunch before the race, at which I learned that our cars – all five of them – had initially failed scrutineering because they had been a few millimetres too long on first inspection. They had been quickly adjusted and had passed when the final measurements were taken.

My duties included the hair-raising experience of flagging the race off from the middle of the track for the first warm-up lap. I say hair-raising, because the first rows on the grid could see that I was there with my enormous flag, but the later ones were busily swinging their cars from side to side to warm up their tyres. Some of them had to take violent action to avoid me. It was a duty I was very glad never to repeat.

The race started in fine style for Jaguar. Jan Lammers, even though he had stressed to his team-mates that he was not going to push the car, soon took the lead. He could overtake any of his opponents on the Mulsanne Straight, at his chosen pace. The pressure he put on Porsche clearly led them into making mistakes. They got into a terrible muddle at the first pit stop by bringing in two cars at exactly the same time. Later on, their leading car inexplicably ran out of fuel on the circuit, and had to be manhandled back to the pits. The leading Jaguar was now a lap ahead.

The two teams spent the first half of the race flat-out, neck and neck, like a rerun of Daytona. After 12 hours we lost our World Champion, Raul Boesel, with a broken gearbox, putting us all on full alert.

Early morning brought our leading car's first setback. A bird had hit and broken the windscreen, which was beginning to collapse in an alarming fashion. Group C cars normally had a screen bonded into the bodyshell, meaning it could not be replaced under race conditions. A broken windscreen would, therefore, have led to withdrawal. But we had standardised our cars so that they complied with both European and IMSA rules, and the latter stipulated that windscreens had to be replaceable.

As a result our screen was held in place by eight nuts and bolts, and our pit team was confident that the windscreen could be replaced whilst still keeping the lead. So it proved: we emerged barely in the lead but – yes –

still leading. The second-placed Porsche also had a minor setback and had drifted two laps behind.

We were beginning to relax, and then it began raining. Hans Stuck, in the leading Porsche, was in his element in the rain, and at these slower rain-induced speeds had no worries about conserving fuel. He began hauling in our leading Jaguar in frightening style. We had a master of the rain also, in Jan Lammers, but he was now asleep. 'Wake him up and get him back in the car,' I suggested to Tom. We did and for the next few hours the race settled down again. The rain stopped and some confidence returned.

For the last driver change, we put Jan back into the car, but his speed inexplicably reduced considerably. Porsche must have also had some problem, because its car did not appreciably gain on us. We anxiously asked Jan how things were going but he clearly did not wish to tell us over the radio.

All he would say was he had a little secret, and then laughed.

When he came into the pits for the last time, he explained he only had fourth gear and was slipping the clutch to enter and leave the pits. Porsche must have had some issue too because their drivers were also conserving their car. We were mightily glad that they did not know that our gearbox might fail if we were put under any pressure, otherwise they would have inevitably tried harder.

We still had three cars in the race and I thought that Tom was being unnecessarily dramatic in marshalling them into formation for the last lap. I nervously asked Tom what he was doing. He immediately replied that he would give the two following cars instructions to push Jan round the circuit if his gearbox failed. With that, this extraordinary race ended.

As soon as Jan was over the line, the crowd spilled onto the track and brought him and our cavalcade to a halt. We had been pursuing our Le Mans goal for four years and now we had won.

I must say that I felt very proud at the presentation ceremony when the national anthem was played and literally thousands of British spectators joined in so enthusiastically. When things had quietened down, I overheard Tom being interviewed by Radio Le Mans. What was it like to win?

'It sure beats losing,' was all that this driven man would say.

Back at team headquarters, I learned that yet again we had no champagne to celebrate our victory. But here at Le Mans, the compound next to ours was occupied by Moët et Chandon. Crates of champagne were soon being passed over the boundary fence, and this time Chloe Smillie allowed her husband to drink it. The team had had no sleep, and as they were drinking their champagne many of them could be seen slipping off to sleep often in mid-sentence. I luckily had a second wind, because I had to be back at Browns Lane first thing in the morning.

It was always a struggle to keep our sponsors. Our racing programme was now costing £12-13 million every year. Castrol, in spite of our great success in the IMSA series in the US, was considering pulling out in 1989. I decided to take the chairman and chief executive and their wives with me and my wife to the Miami Grand Prix, a race we had won in 1988 and one we firmly expected to win in '89. An elaborate display of our racing and marketing expertise had been arranged to try to change Castrol's mind.

The plane set off from London five hours late and so we missed the welcome banquet with our Florida and South Eastern dealers and their wives.

Next day the soft-shell crab lunch went well, and without incident. But our bad luck soon returned.

For the evening, we had hired Al Capone's motor yacht for a trip on the inland waterway, with dinner on board. The yacht ran aground, and we had to be rescued. The rescue tug, after much colourful swearing and pulling and pushing, pronounced us stuck and instructed us to abandon ship. As we were doing just that, the Castrol chief executive, Jonathan Fry, gathered the ladies about him, and flamboyantly led them in singing, 'Abide with Me'…

The following morning the sail from the hotel to the Grand Prix course went without incident, but our jinx was not over. Jaguars were one and two on the grid, but then our number two blew its engine up driving to the starting line. Our number one car then crashed on lap seven. After lunch, we were all too disconsolate to watch the remainder of the race.

Of course, for the return journey, the American Airlines plane was very much delayed. When the plane had eventually taken off, the captain welcomed Sir John Egan and his Jaguar racing team, but only the wives were still awake to acknowledge his welcome. It is a cruel world. We did of course lose the Castrol contract, but I remained good friends with the firm's executives, and in fact the chairman, Lawrence Urquhart, became my non-executive chairman in another company 10 years later.

During 1989, TWR developed a roadgoing version of the XJR-9 that had won Le Mans. Meanwhile, Jim Randle's team in Engineering had created their own V12-powered supercar, and had shown it to great acclaim at the UK motor show.

This project, called XJ220, was handed over to TWR for manufacturing. Tom, in truly entrepreneurial style, shortened it and replaced the V12 with a V6 engine. All the cars to be made were pre-sold, so in the end the exercise was extremely profitable, fully justifying my earlier hopes of the possibility of joint car development. But all of this escaped my close attention. By now I was embroiled in my battle with Ford, to retain the independence of what was a still-emerging and still-growing company.

Chapter 16

Philosophy, leadership and management process

1989-90

Before I joined Jaguar, I had been lucky enough to work in some very good companies and also in some very bad ones. Strangely, the bad companies provided the better learning experience. Stopping bad practice can be done quickly without harm; doing things right takes more time and thought.

I started my working life with Shell, drilling oil wells. Shell were so competent that you felt that the company could do anything it chose to do. It is not always easy to spot why complex organisations work so well. It is only when they are doing difficult and risky things that their form gets easier to spot.

Completing an offshore oil well threatened by a high-pressure blow-out is one such operation. I was a well-site petroleum engineer. The operating manual put the engineer in complete control, so much so that if he was being offered bad advice or instructions from his own superiors who were not on site, he could appeal to higher authority at head office in The Hague and demand an instant reply. It was called a 'Get 'im' telex, meaning 'Get him out of bed'.

Thus the buck stopped absolutely with the engineer. If anything went wrong, it was your fault. This responsibility instils the need to carry out the meticulous pre-planning that crisis management requires. It makes you stand firmly on your own two feet. And for this I was eternally grateful.

Working at British Leyland, on the other hand, showed me how things were done badly. It was pretty easy to spot that this company was not going to work. The leaders never gave the impression that they had a plan. BLMC seemed a hopeless place, with little likelihood of long-term success. The organisational structures and processes were hopelessly intermingled, and a whole posse of people had to be gathered together to fix the simplest of quality problems.

The issues of quality, productivity and shopfloor leadership were not addressed at all. Leadership of the shopfloor seemed to have been handed over to the shop stewards without a fight.

The companies in BL were all the wrong shape, with too many shopfloor workers and too few engineers. Too much money was spent on running inefficient and badly located plants and not enough spent on investment in new products.

The leaders were not creating the opportunities for success but meanwhile were happily delegating the impossible to their subordinates.

From this experience I put together my plan of action for Jaguar – the managerial challenge.

To start with, the biggest challenge for any British manufacturer in 1980 was to get a competitive product to the customer, despite the opposition of the trade union movement and their stormtroopers, the shop stewards. For Jaguar the bar was much higher. Jaguar's products had to be internationally competitive, whereas most UK-manufactured cars went to the home market, where standards and expectations were much lower.

Leadership of the shopfloor had to be wrested from the control of the shop stewards. Most of the operators were in relatively small, highly skilled groups. The 2,000 people on the assembly lines at Browns Lane represented the biggest challenge. I always felt that this battle was there to be won. Our problems were small compared with those at Austin-Morris or Triumph.

We had to build up our engineering department with an extra 1,000 engineers. The simplest way would have been to hire these from other BL companies, but they had mostly known only failure. We also had to introduce Computer Aided Design and modern processes.

Whilst we were busy trying to survive, we were having to set up anew the departments that a car company needs to operate: personnel, finance, purchasing, systems, sales and marketing, public relations and so on. There were huge events happening practically every year: the quality revolutions of 1980, the massive redundancies of 1981, the turnaround, privatisation, the board reconstruction, the model launches. There were only two periods of relative calm during which I could regard Jaguar as a 'going concern'. In such a situation, high-quality, two-way communication was an absolute necessity.

1.Philosophy

A turnaround is mostly about changing people's behaviour, so the leader has to have himself under control. His own behaviour has to be exemplary. It has to be predictable, and not the cause of any confusion. The best self-help book that I have found for this is *Meditations* by Marcus Aurelius, a Roman emperor. He had 20 years to prepare for the biggest job in the world, and put his time to good use. But in a practical sense, a drilling rig is also a good place to learn how to control yourself: ill-tempered words could easily lead to a broken jaw.

It is vital to have goals that are important to you, but not impossible. They should be straightforward enough to share with others. I wanted Jaguar to survive as a healthy company, and certainly to be in better shape than it was when I joined it.

I had been brought up in Coventry. My European office, when I worked for Massey Ferguson, overlooked a school. I remember once seeing about 100 children having a gym lesson, in beautiful disciplined rows. I wondered whether they would ever have jobs. I felt that I possessed the skills to save Jaguar, and doing so would be good for me and good for the community. This goal enabled me to be robust with those who threatened the company's survival, be they shop stewards, poor suppliers, non-executive chairmen or lazy dealers. I did not need to search my soul when hard things needed to be done.

I think it important to have a philosophy driving your actions, something that can help you gather the majority to your cause – those that have tried before and failed, the expert but cynical, the timid, the uncertain. The

---

One of our primary aims was to encourage as many of our employees into training schemes, and we received this award (top left) for our Open Learning Programme. It took many steps to turn Jaguar around but we succeeded in the end. (Philip Porter)

Our advertising agency came up with some great lines, here capitalising on our Sovereign model name. (Philip Porter Archive)

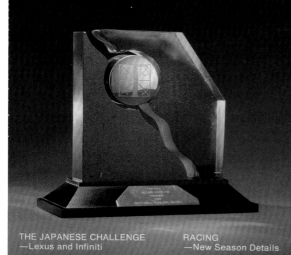

OPEN LEARNING WINS MAJOR AWARD

THE JAPANESE CHALLENGE
—Lexus and Infiniti

RACING
—New Season Details

February 1989

Number 59

The new Jaguar takes high technology into a realm of pure luxury.

Where craftsmen individually select walnut veneers. Leather is hand cut and hand sewn. And every completed car is comprehensively roadtested.

All this takes time. Yet only moments to appreciate.

A turn of the key and up to seven on-board computers inform you of all major functions, via a unique mix of traditional Jaguar instruments and a multi-symbol dot matrix display.

The light alloy 24 valve 3.6 litre electronically fuel injected engine silently achieves 60mph in 7.4 seconds. And reaches an unruffled 136mph'. There's also a new 4 speed automatic transmission.

Handling and refinement surpass even its legendary predecessor, a tribute to tyre and suspension technology proven over 5 million miles. From the frozen wastes of Canada, to the merciless Australian outback.

The anti-dive, anti-squat suspension geometry is enhanced by a self-levelling system, that senses load variables. ABS braking with 'anti-yaw' is standard.

Your well-being is also assured. The air conditioning, has solar-sensing compensation. Seats and door mirrors are power adjusted. The washer jets are electrically heated.

Yet the Sovereign still represents unbeatable value. As do all five new cars, from the 2.9 XJ6 to the opulent Daimler.

Once again, Jaguar have the most sought after currency in the world.

THE NEW JAGUAR SOVEREIGN

The Sovereign. Worth any number of Deutsch marques.

philosophy must also be robust enough to convince yourself, when things look virtually impossible, that what you are doing is right.

My philosophy started with the customer. I believe that in a market economy, the purpose of business is to make money out of satisfying customers. If bankers had concentrated on customer service instead of on their bonuses, which seem to have been mostly gained by encouraging their employees to deceive and cheat their customers, the world would not be in recession and banks would not require such fierce regulation. But for a company making luxury cars, it is self-evident: you will soon run out of customers if you are unable to satisfy them. We concentrated on the quality of our products for the first 12 months – and nothing else. Everybody, even the shop stewards, could support this strategy.

Luckily our inheritance from Bill Lyons and his team was so good that this focus was sufficient for our survival.

Secondly, I believed in our employees. They came to work to give of their best, as almost everybody in the world does. It was our duty to inform, train and lead our employees to a better future, which required us to design better products and give them better equipment and processes. The shop stewards had inherited a powerful hand of cards: mass meetings, picketing and closed shops. We had to win the battle for the hearts and minds of our employees, with little to offer in the short term, and with the shop stewards ready to seize any opportunity to create trouble if they could.

I also believed in the potential of our managers. They often seemed complacent and lacked competence, but nobody had yet tried to show them the way, training them and delegating the possible to them. I was willing to find out how good they could be.

Lastly, I believed that it was my job to build the conditions for success through creating the processes for success. I had to construct a leadership team that was capable of doing the heavy lifting on the major processes, so that we could delegate continuous improvement into the company with a reasonable chance of success. For example, we could never have succeeded if we had not got full control over the Castle Bromwich body and paint plant, and over our suppliers and dealers. We could not design new products without resources similar to our competitors. We had to find out how world-class companies did things, and do likewise. Above all, we had to delegate the do-able into the organisation.

I felt that if I were doing these things, I was not only doing my best, but doing the best that could be done, so I could pursue my programme with utmost vigour.

2. Leadership and management

'Know the way, show the way' is a handy dictum. From Day One I created a management team that possessed all the information available, and took all the decisions together. As much as possible, I shared my authority. We did very little that did not have consensus, but I was tyrannical in expecting everybody to abide by the decisions we made. In the early years, we were constantly in so much peril that we had no other way.

We very quickly drew the top 100 managers into a cohesive group, making sure that this group understood what we were doing, and why. Many of the key decisions we took were debated in the group: the big 1981 redundancy programme, launching XJ40, whether to have a tobacco company as lead sponsor of our Le Mans racing programme. Later, when I talked to members of this group, they often said it was the best period of their managerial careers.

From the very start, all senior managers knew what our German competitors could achieve, because we told them, emphasising that it was our collective task to do as well as they did. The strategy was to be internationally competitive in everything we did.

The other vitally important key group we singled out was the first-line supervisors and foremen. We had to understand fully their difficulties and what they were capable of delivering. For most of our employees, this group constituted their day-to-day management. We had to train them, coach them and inspire them – but also listen to them and befriend them. It was the duty of all the 'top 100' managers to behave towards the first-line supervisors in this way.

3. Processes

Until the arrival of TQM, all our processes were mostly home-made or inherited from BL, in which case they had mostly come secondhand from Ford. Despite this heritage, many of the things that a car company needs to do we ended up doing very well.

On a worldwide basis our sales and marketing teams were outstanding, consistently choosing dealers who gave quality service to their customers. They stressed treating the customer as an individual, and when spending money on the customer they made sure he or she got something special from it. Better to give a customer a musical evening with dinner in a stately home than a glimpse of a TV advert. Dealers took their customers to support the racing teams, dealers and customers together creating a family atmosphere. Shared advertising with the dealers not only made the money go further, but helped to emphasise that same family atmosphere. We tended to innovate in the US and UK, and then spread the word elsewhere.

Our PR programmes were probably 'best in class'. We started with motoring and local media, allowing our story of a successful British car company to speak for itself. Always we were courteous and helpful. We were clearly far too small to have extensive advertising budgets, so we let our story sell the cars.

Communication with our employees was done well and created a positive atmosphere, which allowed us to manage our manufacturing process improvements. This gave us a chance to survive. Programmes such as Hearts and Minds and Open Learning, and the US Dealer Awards and Twenty-Five Year Awards, where we presented gold watches at evening supper events, were all inventive, well executed and engendered a family atmosphere. Mike Beasley and I tried to shake everybody's hand at Christmas time, always trying to give meaning to the work experience. We had created a freedom to manage which any manager from the '60s and '70s would have deeply envied. Certainly Bill Lyons was very impressed.

The process improvements themselves were so successful in reducing the man-hours to manufacture the XJ6 from 700 hours per car to 300 hours that they underpinned the spectacular improvement in productivity.

Trouble-shooting our suppliers' problems had gone well, but we had not made them self-reliant and they did get into trouble again, when we launched the XJ40. Where we had not done so well was in new product development, in our own design work and that of our suppliers, in introduction of the new products into manufacturing, and in planning our testing programmes. I also felt that we were unlikely to achieve our competitors' levels of productivity. I had still not managed to get people to work on the assembly lines right up to and including the last hour of the day.

For all these reasons, the management team led Jaguar into embracing TQM. It was a controversial decision, which I tried to make sure was supported universally, but not everyone was completely convinced. With TQM, we gained a body of knowledge through the work of Edwards Deming and the experience of our consultants.

I was immediately struck by a comparison between a European and a process-controlled Japanese new product launch, as they described it.

Diagram 1. European product launch.

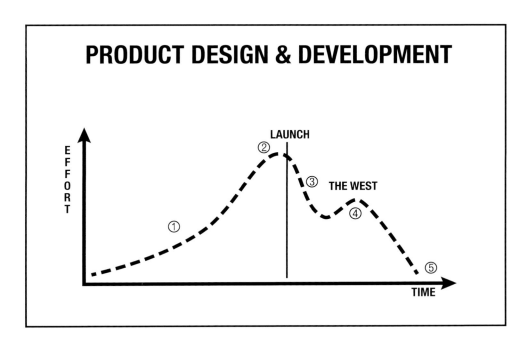

Notes.
1. Considerable work done before decision taken to proceed. Many new part numbers created after putting parts out to competitive tender.
2. Peak output of new part numbers just before production start-up.
3. New part numbers continue after production start-up, to overcome manufacturing problems.
4. Adverse customer experience requires a whole raft of new parts.
5. Car in good condition 18 months after launch.
6. 2.75 parts designed for every part in eventual car.

Diagram 2. Japanese process-controlled launch.

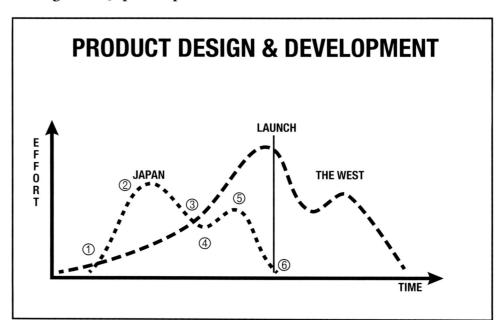

Notes.
1. First nine months spent on Quality Function Deployment, describing every component and its performance compared to previous components and those of competition. Every part number has a life and a process leader of its own. The decision to go ahead with the new car is taken in full knowledge of its competitive position and where the weaknesses are and thus where design effort must go.
2. Design car, together with suppliers, all at the same time.
3. Build prototypes on production equipment, design new parts for improved manufacturing performance.
4. Test car built according to production processes. (We were able to add this phase into our traditional European approach, because our existing XJ6 was selling so well.)
5. Design new parts after testing.
6. Launch car. Car in good customer condition at launch. 1.30 parts designed for every part in launch vehicle, twice the productivity of the European process.

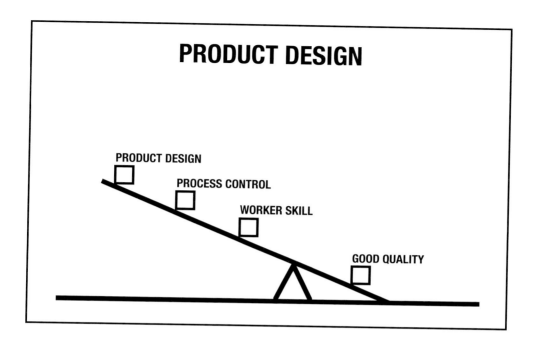

PRODUCT DESIGN

PRODUCT DESIGN
PROCESS CONTROL
WORKER SKILL
GOOD QUALITY

The second illustration demonstrates the importance of design on final quality and thus on customer satisfaction. Design, along with process controls, is of course far more important than operator skill, which is most commonly blamed for poor quality.

The purpose of management is to get large groups of people to work in harmony together. How much more productive that will be if everyone can bring their enthusiasm and brains to work, as well as their hands and feet. This requires controlled and effective delegation, which in turn requires processes which are designed to work and are manned by a workforce trained to make them work, and also to improve upon them. For example, if every team or process leader is trained to do simple engineering drawings and process-change instructions, teams can put forward solutions to problems rather than just flag them up. An organisation can deal with many more potential solutions than it can potential problems.

Myron Tribus and his colleagues had a good grounding in the car business and came with conceptual solutions to our problems with design, and the associated co-ordination with manufacturing and suppliers. We had in the main been trying to do the right things but without the precision required to be world-best in every key thing we did. World-best was what Jaguar had to be – anything less simply would not do.

In TQM it is important to be extremely clear and precise in stating your objectives, simply because then you are quite likely to achieve them. Do not try to achieve the unnecessary, as this might equally be achieved, needlessly wasting effort.

Jaguar chose to be the best luxury car company in the world by creating the highest possible customer satisfaction at the lowest possible cost. These seemingly conflicting objectives can be handled by good process design. In any event, this is what really has to be done to beat your competitors.

Once you have decided on your objectives, it is then necessary to be equally clear on how they are to be achieved. In Jaguar's case, this was by:

1. Measuring customer satisfaction and comparing this with the performance of major competitors.
2. Continuously measuring and improving every process of design, manufacture, purchase, service and sales.
3. Allowing every employee to give of his or her best through listening, leadership and training.

It is also important to be very clear about how you expect every employee to behave. What are the good things you expect employees to do? What are the things they should not do? Where are the grey areas on which you would expect employees to seek advice from their supervisors?

We were in the middle of constructing our detailed mission statement including all the above when the attention of our management committee was diverted by our efforts to fight off the Ford bid. From a personal point of view, in future jobs I was able to use these powerful ideas successfully, to improve the performance of airports, construction projects, property companies and water companies. I am saddened when I see vastly important institutions such as the National Health Service get into the hands of politicians.

Targets are wildly thrown at the organisation with no idea of the processes that will be used to achieve them and whether the resources exist that might make them possible. It is a management truism that people try to achieve what they are instructed to achieve, but they might very well ignore everything else. When waiting times were thrown at the NHS as their main objective, it was predictable that they might be achieved but the fact that some hospitals would rather let you die than keep you waiting seemed not to be predictable to the unseeing politicians.

Until the NHS is given the objective of maximising patient welfare at the percentage of GDP that we can afford, it is highly unlikely that this muddle-headed political interference in its affairs can be brought to a useful conclusion.

Returning to the subject of Jaguar, I felt that we were making good progress with Myron and his TQM colleagues and I could see a sparkle in the eyes of people as they grasped the power of these ideas.

It was deeply troubling to have to turn aside and to start repelling the Ford executives who were attempting to board our ship.

Chapter 17

The Ford takeover

1989-90

After Alex Trotman had thrown his bomb into our midst, I gathered the Jaguar management team together to create our response to Ford's approach. As a team we had faced many crises threatening Jaguar's survival, and up to now we had found a solution to every one. This crisis, however, felt very different. Ford had now come back at us for the third time. There was unlikely to be an easy way out.

I opened up the meeting by describing my unusual encounter with Alex Trotman. He had lectured me and clearly had not been interested in much that I had to say. He was not the slightest bit put off by potentially losing the company's existing management in the event of a takeover. He was buying a nameplate and some assets, and he had not been much interested in what we had achieved or even what we needed. Much less had he been interested in our plans for the future.

Mike Beasley, who had worked for Ford, said that they only knew the Ford way and they would make us as much like Ford as they could.

Roger Putnam, meanwhile, pointed out that this was not our only option. Bob Eaton, the GM-Europe president, had intimated to him recently that General Motors were still interested in some relationship short of overall ownership.

John Edwards said that he would update his defence documents. But any share-buying by Ford would have to satisfy a dual set of conditions, the most immediate and useful of which were incorporated in the US Hart Scott Rodino Act. This had been put in place to protect United States companies from dawn raids on their shares by predators. The Act stated that substantial companies with US sales of more than $100 million had to be given 30 days' notice before any US predator, at least, could buy any shares. This was intended to enable the victim to put its defence in place before it was too late to protect itself.

Of course, under UK rules, no predator could buy more than 15 per cent of our shares without the permission of the holder of the Golden Share, the Secretary of State for Trade and Industry, who at this time was Nicholas Ridley. That Golden Share was in place until at least mid-1991. We, therefore, had some time to defend ourselves, or so we thought.

No US company could buy any shares for 30 days, and then for at least two more years it would be prevented from increasing its shareholding beyond 15 per cent.

Our conclusions were that Ford was the least acceptable owner. It was not used to having arms-length relationships with subsidiaries. Jaguar had almost died from attempts to make it an integrated part of BL and being absorbed by Ford could only lead to the same fate. We decided we should redouble our efforts to find a more suitable partner or partners. We should recommence talks with General Motors as a slightly safer partner, and as a matter of urgency seek other partners who perhaps could help us to make Jaguar ownership too expensive for Ford to contemplate.

We put these conclusions to our board, now strengthened by the addition of John Baring, chairman of the bank of that name. George Magan also joined us for our deliberations.

The defence position we put forward was a mixed one. The US, our major market, was going into recession and our sales were declining, but in the rest of the world sales were still growing. XJ40 quality was rapidly improving, and sales were going well. The new XJ-S convertible was selling very well everywhere in the world. Costs and productivity were improving. Our new-model programme now included an F-type, a very exciting new V8 engine and a facelift for the XJ40.

On the downside, we assumed that the rest of the world would soon follow the US into recession. The dollar was very weak and the pound strong, as a result of the UK Government's policy of using high interest rates to control inflation. For the foreseeable future, profits would thus be weak and we would have to borrow money if we wanted to push forward with our model programme.

In the short term, our own financial performance would not protect us from predators. We also predicted that as Nicholas Ridley was a dry-as-dust capitalist, we would not get an extension to our Golden Share period. Under pressure from Ford would we even get our full period of Golden Share protection? This was one question we had to consider. We were alive and well, but too small to protect ourselves. This was a position shared by many British companies and for which no government had invented a solution until this one, with its Golden Share. But would they use it to protect us?

Ford had been in Britain longer than Jaguar and were now the number one car manufacturer in the United Kingdom. Consequently, they were much more important to the UK than Jaguar.

The board endorsed our strategy: no deal with Ford, start talks with General Motors and seek other partners. The board made one other very strong point, which was that we should not have any further discussions with Ford of Europe. If Ford really wanted to talk with us, we would only talk with the chairman of the parent Ford Motor Company in the US – and with nobody at all if they threatened to buy our shares.

The next move in the drama was a piece of pure theatre. On schedule, straight after the board meeting, Alex Trotman rang up and asked what the board had concluded.

'They said, "No, Jaguar is not for sale",' I told him, adding that I had already warned him that this was what they would say.

'In that case, we are going to start buying your shares tomorrow,' he replied.

'I wouldn't do that,' I said. 'You'll find that buying our shares is illegal, and we will demand that you reverse the transactions.'

When Trotman queried how it could be illegal, when Jaguar shares were freely bought and sold on the Stock Exchange, I explained about the Hart Scott Rodino Act and how Ford would be obliged to give 30 days' notice before buying any shares. He immediately asked what we would do when we received such a notice, to which I replied that UK regulations would oblige us to inform the London Stock Exchange of the impending purchases. He realised that this was likely to mean that the share price would then rise.

'Well, I think that was what Hart Scott Rodino had in mind,' I said. 'We will get some protection, and we do know that there are others interested in protecting our independence. I must tell you some of the board's other conclusions. Because your intentions are so serious, it only wishes me to have further talks with you if you withdraw your threat of buying our shares and, if there are to be further talks, they must be with your US chairman and not with anyone representing Ford of Europe. I am sure you understand why. We value our independence. We have struggled hard for it and don't intend to give it up without a fight.'

With that the conversation ended and for the moment communication with Ford ceased. We got on with working on alternative schemes. In particular, Roger Putnam led the discussions with GM. Bob Eaton had already given the matter a great deal of thought and had come up with a concept which he felt played to the strengths of both organisations.

GM felt they could not profitably expand into the executive car market, although they did have a concept car, and engine and manufacturing facilities. Jaguar already had a concept car in the form of a project called XJ80. The General Motors idea was that XJ80 would use a floorpan, engine and some other components from GM and be manufactured at the Opel plant at Rüsselsheim. It would then be sold to a Jaguar/GM joint venture for distribution. The distribution would be by GM in Europe and by Jaguar for the UK, the United States, and the 'Rest of the World'.

The whole process would be owned by a joint 50/50 venture between GM and Jaguar. Essentially the capital Jaguar needed for the investment would be provided by a rights issue underwritten by GM.

There are no short cuts for a programme of this size. The only way we could decide whether it would be profitable was to design the car. Overall design would be a Jaguar responsibility, but much of the detail would be done by GM, who would also be responsible for all the manufacturing engineering and purchasing.

The project was full of peril for Jaguar. The car itself had to be a success, and we were still grappling with the processes for 'right first time' engineering on our own account, never mind doing it in a joint venture with another company. What would our European distributors think of GM selling Jaguars alongside their own products? What would our workforce think of GM building Jaguars in Germany? Worst of all, how vulnerable would Jaguar become in the coming recession and would this project make us even more vulnerable?

This was by no means the perfect lifeline, but at that time it was the only lifeline we had.

The massive undertaking of designing the car was started purposefully and in good harmony with the Opel engineers. They seemed to get on well with Jim Randle and his team of 'skunk' engineers, who were doing the whole project off-line, so that it did not upset our existing new-model programme.

Together with George Magan, now with his own investment bank, Hambro Magan, we began searching for friends who would help to preserve our independence. Two very important allies emerged who could under certain circumstances help to create a blocking group. Our distributor in Japan, the Seibu Saison Group, very quickly offered to help, as did Anthony Bamford of JCB. We knew that a lot of our US shareholders were 'deep safe' investors, and would remain loyal to the board. Together with our distributors and Jaguar directors and employees, we could make it very expensive indeed for Ford to attempt a takeover.

We were much buoyed up by all this activity and were beginning to feel that, in the middle of this mêlée, a solution would emerge.

On one of my trips to North America, Roger Smith, the chairman of GM, suggested we meet to review progress on our joint venture. I explained some of my misgivings to him. He was, however, quite reassuring about the GM position and positive that full ownership was not his company's intention: they were there to help. I was of course deeply sceptical of large and small companies trying to run joint programmes. It was at this juncture that I pointed out to him that when an elephant gets into bed with a mouse it may not be very interesting for the elephant, but the mouse usually gets killed.

Ford also contacted us and said that Don Petersen, their US chairman, would like to open up discussions on a clean-sheet-of-paper basis, to discuss possible co-operation. Don courteously listened to me and John Edwards,

---

Top left: From 1990, the Ford Motor Company ruled Jaguar and thus our company had a new sovereign. Top right: With the departure of Hamish Orr-Ewing, we appointed John Baring, chairman of Barings Bank and a director of the Bank of England, a non-executive director.

The Jaguar range – XJ6, XJ12 and XJ-S – when Ford took over the reins and I decided to seek fresh challenges. (Jon Pressnell Collection)

Today, Britain has
a new Sovereign.

and we were able to tell him of our progress and aspirations.

I sensed that if we might, after all, end up with Ford, this was the time to negotiate the best possible deal. He was honest and firm: the relationship must lead to full ownership. I knew that with these huge businesses these interim deals only worked on a purely temporary basis. The inevitable ebb and flow of people and events would change everything. How long would Don be chairman? How long would our performance keep the Ford machine off our backs?

I was used to winning outright on this Jaguar venture. The game could still be won, I felt. So let us carry on kicking the ball down the field. Was this the best use of our Golden Share safety period – letting Ford, in our view the worst possible owners, into a cosy relationship in return for their 15 per cent initial shareholding?

Don, however, would not take 'no' for an answer. He suggested that John Edwards and John Grant of Ford work together on formulating processes that would enable Jaguar and Ford to work fruitfully together and we would all meet in Washington a few weeks later. This meeting did take place, but John and I reiterated our intention to remain independent. Don on his part promised to leave us alone for a while, which he did for several months.

Detroit is a small place and word of our possible co-operation with General Motors must have got around, because Ford clearly became very nervous. The next act in the drama unfolded with savage intensity. The Hart Scott Rodino declaration from Ford landed on my desk in early 1989. Our immediate declaration to the Stock Exchange triggered not only a rise in our shares from £4.05 to £6.00, but also widespread interest elsewhere.

BMW offered to help in our share-support operation, and further offers of interest came in from Fiat, Renault, Mercedes-Benz and Volvo. I also took a telephone call from Lee Iacocca of Chrysler asking if he should throw his hat into the ring. I warned him that it would all be too expensive for him.

Practically every investment bank in London was representing one car company or another and everyone was getting excited. The share price rose remorselessly.

John Edwards and I had calculated that if all our new product developments, including the GM joint venture, went well, and we emerged satisfactorily from the recession – and the dollar rose above $1.50 to the pound – the most we could envisage Jaguar shares being worth was £6.50. The share price quickly exceeded this level, and we felt that at this price we could no longer ask our friends to buy shares. We were thrown by the frenzy of activity in the market.

Hambro Magan reported that British institutions were selling their shares and short-term speculators were buying, to the point where soon they would dominate our share register. This mêlée was obviously not working to our advantage.

The only port of call left was General Motors. John and I made a Concorde day trip to New York. On the way over, John described to me the increasing acrimony creeping into the discussions with GM-Europe. The performance clauses being insisted on by the GM negotiators were becoming increasingly onerous for Jaguar and we seemed more like protagonists than potential joint-venture partners.

When we met Roger Smith, he was reassuring about the collaboration being a priority, and said that he still wanted to go ahead. However, he warned us that he was not going to get into a bidding war with Ford.

It was becoming clear to me that shareholders might have to choose between two very different deals: outright sale to Ford, or the joint venture plus perhaps a 20 per cent rights issue to GM.

The GM deal would only work if we continued to be protected by the Golden Share.

On the way back to the UK, John and I became convinced that the GM deal would be difficult to sell to our shareholders. We could not pretend it was worth more than it was and the share price was already higher than that.

We decided to reopen talks with Ford. Perhaps they would settle for a holding position, with the various rival bidders all holding positions up to the 15 per cent allowed by the Golden Share.

A Ford deal of some kind might be the only viable outcome, and might indeed be better than a risky project with GM, cobbled together in haste and with a degree of acrimony.

Unbeknown to us, Ford already had a team in Sweden to sign a deal with Saab, and in 24 more hours that is what would have happened. I arranged another Concorde day trip to New York, this time to begin discussions with Ford. We had finally agreed that open-ended discussions could start.

These had barely started when I had a telephone call from Nicholas

Ridley. It was very short and very alarming.

'I am announcing in Parliament this afternoon that I am removing the Golden Share from Jaguar and this will allow commercial negotiations for the future of Jaguar to take place with all interested parties,' he told me.

'I am therefore instructing that all dealings in your shares will be suspended at the London Stock Exchange at noon today, until I have made the announcement.'

I was mortified but not completely surprised. Ridley was, as I say, a dry-as-dust capitalist. I said he was being extremely discourteous in giving us only 20 minutes' notice and told him he should not suspend our shares.

'Well, that is what I am doing, and that's that,' he replied, and rang off.

If he had been polite enough to listen, I would have told him that trading would still be taking place on the NASDAQ exchange in New York, where about 50 per cent of our shares were held. There the share price roared ahead, at one point touching £9.00 per share.

But for Jaguar, it was collapse of stout party. We had nowhere else to go.

The negotiations were very quickly concluded, with Ford making an agreed formal offer of £8.50 per share to Jaguar shareholders, for all the outstanding shares. This valued Jaguar in total at £1.6 billion.

Jaguar shareholders had received an annual return of 27 per cent, if they had bought their shares at the flotation price of £1.65. Ford could have bought the company for virtually nothing if they had done so when I arrived in 1980.

I personally felt extremely sad.

It was almost as if part of my soul had been taken away. I reasoned, however, that Ford had a long-term commitment to the UK and that as they had paid so much for the company, maybe they would look after it.

I had started on my journey wanting the survival of Jaguar. What would Ford ownership mean for that survival plan?

That was my only consideration.

I would find out in due course, when the people at Ford had made up their minds on what they wanted to do with Jaguar.

Was there anything I could do to help them be positive in their approach to the company?

I had to find out.

Postscript

lmost immediately after the transaction had been completed, I was invited to go to Ford World Headquarters in Dearborn. I wondered what to expect. Was I being brought over to Rome as if I were a captured British chieftain, to be taunted, poked at and humiliated? After all, my actions had been expensive for the men from Ford, and they had every right to do so. They were now in charge.

None of that. I met with almost total indifference. The only person showing any interest at all was the new chairman, 'Red' Poling. He had replaced the chairman I had negotiated with, Don Petersen, who had retired – although one director intimated he had been pushed.

Poling called me into his office. He was friendly enough, but anxious and perplexed. With very little preamble, he said, 'Say John, what am I going to tell my shareholders? I've paid five times book value for a car company. I can't think of any car company worth even book value.'

I tried to be helpful. 'Well, when I was taught to be a salesman, I was taught to sell the sizzle not the sausage. What you have bought here is $500 million of sausage, but you also bought $2 billion worth of sizzle. Think about it.'

Behind my seemingly amusing reply was a very profound idea, which I hoped 'Red' would get his mind around. At Jaguar, we had recreated a company worth much more than its assets. We had found that, as long as we could deliver our customers with products up to their expectations, we could charge more for them than Ford could for its products.

Customers valued association with the brand, which they rated much more highly than they did Ford. We had worked hard at it, with our turn-round story, our education system, our products, our racing, our marketing programmes, our choice of dealers, even our racing-inspired XJ220. The $2 billion of sizzle was just as real as the $500 million of sausage.

'Red' shook his head in disbelief. 'Well, I'll be damned,' he said, and with that we parted.

I only stayed at Jaguar for a few months. I did try to inculcate some affection in the Ford people for the company they had paid so much money for, but it was a fairly hopeless task. As far as they were concerned, they had bought a nameplate and some assets. The first people they sent could not imagine that there was anything else to find but the assets, and they did not like the assets. One of the early arrivals described some of the facilities as worse than at Gorky, a car plant he had seen in Russia.

The Toyota visitors, when they had seen the same 30-year-old facilities, had seen a motivated workforce doing their best, with great enthusiasm. Ford did not seek out the men and women who had created the sizzle; as these people did not appear on the balance sheet, they reasoned that they must not exist at all.

I have often been asked what sort of job Ford did for Jaguar. My reply would be that they did an honest job of making Jaguar part of Ford. They did a very capable job of installing their quality processes into everything that Jaguar did to design and manufacture their products, and certainly these processes did create better-quality cars. Their new cars looked like Jaguars but they did not allow the style to move on.

Bill Lyons had been a leader in design, not a follower. Ford stuck rigidly to this perceived heritage – which was in fact no such thing. Worse, with the small X-type Jaguar they fell into the nameplate trap and arguably created a Ford that looked like a Jaguar.

But they did not run away easily. They invested billions of pounds into the company and lost billions of pounds running it, especially during the recession of the early 1990s. They knew about sausage and spent a lot of money creating more sausage – but without much sizzle. There was good honest endeavour, but no early effort to add glamour to a glamorous marque. The attempt they made to add glamour by investing in a Jaguar Formula 1 team was simply a purchased service that cost a lot of money and was never competitive enough, or close enough to the brand, to add value.

To do better, someone over a long period of time needed to have loved the Jaguar marque and been passionate about trying to make the best cars in the world, nothing less. I detected that at times someone at Ford was getting the message, because the XK8 was a very fine car indeed and the XKR, with its supercharged V8 engine, was one of the best cars I have ever driven. Great cars do sell well and the XK8 sold well. Ford could have done better if they had consistently gone for this high standard, as Bill Lyons and his team had always tried to do.

It is not possible for a huge volume-car company like Ford to run a small luxury-car company like Jaguar with 'business as usual'. The instincts of Ford people did not line up with the long-term requirements of trying to make the best luxury cars in the world. There was a constant flow of Ford managers going through Jaguar. Sometimes they got it right, like the XK8, but their volume-car instincts, together with an empty factory at Halewood, led them into the X-type trap, where making a small Ford look like a Jaguar debased the whole range.

In the end, I was right about US companies. As soon as its own business in North America was under threat, Ford did indeed abandon its now loss-making luxury brand and moved it on. It was a distraction. Back in Detroit, they had real work to do, putting their own house in order.

Could we have avoided being taken over? It is a question I have often pondered.

No matter how well we could have done, even if we had made no mistakes, we could not have created a value too big for Ford's purse. As Alex Trotman said when we first met, 'We have $7.5 billion dollars in the bank. Everything is for sale.' The only thing that could have saved us would have been if the Government had rigidly adhered to the Golden Share and its long-term retention, which it was not prepared to do.

Sir Jackie Stewart helped with the development of the XK8, working alongside the Jaguar engineers. He was also the man who recommended Tom Walkinshaw to me. (Philip Porter Archive)

In 2000 Ford made the decision to enter Formula 1, branding the team with the Jaguar name. Proving big companies cannot run F1 teams, it was an embarrassing failure. (Philip Porter Archive)

I do think that governments should give earnest consideration again to using Golden Shares to protect important companies that are too small to be protected by their own share price.

Would my team have done any better if we had not been taken over? Of course, we will never know. The 1990s recession was much worse than I had predicted and we would have had a very difficult time. Survival would have been the issue, especially with all those disgruntled shareholders if we had turned down £8.50 per share. We would not have had the luxury of being able to lose money. I suspect, however, that my objective of Jaguar's healthy survival was better served by Ford's relatively benign ownership during the very difficult times of the early '90s rather than by staying independent. It is true that we had faced much worse problems in the '80s, and my suspicion is that we would have muddled through, somehow or other, as Bill Lyons always did. But it is doubtful that we could have continued investing heavily in a new-model programme.

Now the future for Jaguar looks much brighter. Tata have turned out to be excellent owners.

When Lindsey Halstead, the chairman of Ford of Europe, first visited Jaguar, one employee asked how long Ford would own the company. He clearly did not want to be drawn into any commitment but he ventured a reply. 'A very long time,' he said. 'At least 10 or 15 years.' That turned out to be about right.

The same employee put the identical question to Ratan Tata when he came to Jaguar for the first time. 'Why, for ever!' was his reply.

If you want to make the best cars in the world – and for Jaguar there can be no other aspiration – then that is the only answer.

The XK8, and sister XKR, were cars I rated highly; this proved that Ford could build good Jaguars but sadly it was the exception to the rule. (Philip Porter)

The previously leaping Jaguar was not a happy animal under its new masters, as some wag illustrated in this period cartoon. (John Egan Archive)

THE NEW LOGO

Index

Saving Jaguar